ROCK FACE
Techniques of rock climbing

ROCK FACE

Techniques of rock climbing
RON JAMES

British Broadcasting Corporation

The television programmes
First broadcast on BBC-1 January to March 1974
Re-broadcast on BBC-1 September to December 1974
The series produced by John Dobson

Acknowledgment is due to the following for permission to reproduce photographs
HOWELL EVANS plate 24; JOHN EYNON plates 23, 38 and 56; JOHN
WILKINSON front cover; KEN WILSON plate 46. The remaining photographs
were taken by RON & BARBARA JAMES.

Apart from my general thanks to the many instructors, guides, clients and
pupils who have shared in the development of the techniques described
in this book, special thanks for daring to dispute points and probe
statements must go to Dave Bland, Dave Siviter, John Brailsford and
students of the I. M. Marsh College rock-climbing specialist groups.
    Valerie Siviter typed the manuscript, and David Owen, of Bangor,
gave considerable technical help with photographs.
    Barbara, my wife, took many of the photographs, and posed for many
others, and was also closely involved in the writing.

R.J.

Published to accompany a series of programmes prepared in
consultation with the BBC Further Education Advisory Council

© Ron James and the British Broadcasting Corporation 1974

First published 1974
Reprinted 1974

Published by the British Broadcasting Corporation
35 Marylebone High Street, London W1M 4AA
Printed in England by Lowe & Brydone (Printers) Ltd. Thetford Norfolk

ISBN 0 563 10802 9

CONTENTS

PREFACE

Sooner or later everyone asks the same question about climbing—'Why do you do it?' And indeed when the layman sits in front of his television set and sees a climber soaked to the skin, chilled to the marrow and clinging on desperately with his fingertips, the question seems entirely justified.

It was Mallory who produced the classic reply – 'I climb a mountain because it's there'. This is a neat answer, but not entirely convincing.

I've talked to many climbers, and they've all tied themselves into verbal knots, talking about challenge and achievement, ambience, atmosphere and danger. Not one of them has produced a satisfactory answer.

The author of this book, Ron James, and his wife Barbara, have also covered unpublished reams of paper to the same end.

In making ten programmes for our series *Rockface* I have made remarkably inexpert assisted passages up and down many routes. At the end of it all the only answer to the question I can suggest is this – try it for yourself. When you suddenly realise that you've actually made it to the top of your first climb you'll begin to understand why, and want to do it all over again.

John Dobson

This book sets out to encompass the details of methods and techniques developed over thousands of feet of climbing and teaching and argued out over innumerable cups of tea or pints of ale. Perhaps the biggest problem has been what to leave out, for in almost every technique alternatives exist of various merits. However, I have tried to steer a middle course and to indicate the principles involved at each stage rather than to dogmatise about the perfect knot, the only way of clipping in to a sling, or one particular body position for a certain move.

My problem was whether to write it for the armchair climber unable as he is to feel rock or handhold or rope, or must I consider my expert friends who will be the ones to face me with subtle criticisms? At the back of my mind I saw myself at fourteen with new nailed boots and rope, seconded and encouraged by two slightly concerned parents. Happily they understood, for my father rode rather fast motor bikes whilst my mother would have been a Channel swimmer. This city dwelling trio really needed a book like this and I feel that if I have written a book which could have helped them, then it would serve equally its other readers too. Deciding how to present a book of this nature in a short space of time, from thoughts gathered over many years, made me feel more nervous and apprehensive than I ever feel at the foot of a rock climb.

Although the chapters are written in a certain order, this is not necessarily an outline of the development of a climber. Certainly 'abseiling' may be practised earlier whilst 'starting to lead' is so critical a stage, its placing is more a feeling than a definite step in a progression.

Finally the most important thing about both rock climbing and indeed mountaineering is that it gives pleasure. No book can convey this, yet I hope that this great sport which has given me some of the finest moments in my life and many wonderful days, will give this pleasure to you, the readers. Good climbing!

Ron James

1 THE CHALLENGE OF ROCK

This book is about the sport of rock climbing as practised on the mountains, outcrops and sea cliffs of Britain. Although many of the techniques are used also in Alpine climbing or winter expeditions on snow and ice, no attempt has been made to cover the special skills and dangers involved in these other aspects of the greater sport of mountaineering, of which rock climbing is but a part.

Historically, rock climbing developed in the Alps as a means of overcoming more difficult mountains or of taking more difficult ways up mountains already climbed by normal methods. In Britain, climbing rocks was a way of practising for these harder Alpine climbs. Abroad, reaching the summit of the peak was usually the aim of a rock climb, but in Britain it rapidly became acceptable simply to climb a rockface by a certain route and then return to the base of the face and to climb it again by yet another route.

In the early days of British rock climbing, the climbers followed the Alpine idea of taking the easiest ridges and buttresses to reach the summits. However, as steeper faces were attempted, the need for some security away from exposure to height was felt, and so they climbed the obvious rifts on the faces – the gullies. Some of these gullies still provide hard problems for the techniques needed are not now popular. Today, climbing greasy rounded rocks and wearing nailed boots is not as attractive as it was seventy years ago.

Once the brute force struggling of the gulley era had conquered the majority of these odious places, the climber developed techniques to ascend the more open areas of rock, the slabs and walls between the gullies. Footwork replaced arm strength and rhythmic balance climbing succeeded strenuous wriggling. Climbers still followed obvious lines, be they cracks and chimneys or slabs, but they became accustomed to exposure and ventured on to faces and walls previously considered impossible.

Each improvement in technique or equipment in succeeding decades, each infusion of new blood with different attitudes to the sport, has led to harder and steeper faces being climbed until now, most possible pieces of rock in England and Wales, and many in Scotland, have been climbed by many routes. Every popular cliff of good rock near a city or easily accessible by road, whether it is twenty or a thousand feet high, has been covered with a network of routes, often within feet of each other and it is rare to visit one of these crags on a fine Saturday without finding numerous climbers in action. Most of the climbs are named, described and illustrated in hundreds of guide books, supplements and magazine articles.

For many people, the sport of rock climbing has become a means in itself, particularly on the smaller outcrops near cities and on some of our sea cliffs. Perhaps this is the most recent revolution, for until twenty years ago, it was considered rather poor if one did not think of outcrop climbing simply as a means of preparing for climbing on mountain crags – and even that was only justified as a preparation for Alpine mountaineering. Today, outcrop gymnastics is a sport in itself, certainly as valuable and rewarding to the enthusiast as an Alpine snow-plod is to the classic mountaineer.

Ideally, a person should come to rock climbing after an apprenticeship of hill walking and scrambling. In this period he would learn to understand something about mountains, their weather and their moods, to use map and compass, identify various rocks, feel rhythmic movement and acquire a basic fitness and relationship with the wild environment that would make crags sympathetic places to visit. In hill walking the hands are rarely used, and danger comes more from the weather than the mountain; but in scrambling a fatal fall can occur, handholds and footholds need to be selected and tested with care, and so some of the basic problems of rock climbing can be encountered.

Danger is a part of rock climbing and for many, one of its

attractions. Modern equipment and techniques make it now much safer than it was, even a decade ago, but some risk still exists. With experience comes judgement and skill, so it is possible to attempt more difficult climbs. It is the ability to select the right target for the day's climb which is the greatest skill of all. Select too low a target and the climber will feel unextended and slightly dissatisfied. Pick one too hard and the gentlest reward will be a nasty scare or a deflating retreat, the harshest could be serious injury or death.

Before each climb, a climber must do a simple sum:

$$\text{T} = \text{A} + \text{P} + \text{E}.$$

He cannot select the target (T) until he has assessed the other three factors. A – Ability, skill, strength, size and experience of his party. He must discover whether they have climbed a climb of this difficulty before. Are there too many or too few in the team? Can they use the rope so as to protect both the leader and each other? Do they understand the techniques involved? Are he and his team mentally and physically fit and prepared for this route? Next, he must consider P, the prevailing conditions. Is the rock dry or wet and greasy, so increasing the difficulty? Will the weather change? Have they enough time, even allowing for errors and unexpected difficulty? Do they know exactly where the climb goes? Finally, he must examine critically the third factor, E, the equipment available. Have they enough rope of the right type? Have they sufficient slings, pitons and so on? Have all the party got the correct footwear, headgear, clothing and emergency equipment? Only after considering these factors and adding them together can a suitable target be selected.

No book can hope to replace the right experience or good judgement but all of the above factors are simple to assess and it is with this aim in mind that this book hopes to help aspirant climbers and leaders to be able to answer many of the questions involved in the above sum.

Although the basic aim of better equipment, increased skill and better training can be to make climbers safer, the real aim is to extend their limits so that harder targets may be attempted, with enjoyment, at all levels of the sport.

BASIC CLIMBING TECHNIQUE

JUST MOVING

In chapter one, the value of hill walking and scrambling as an introduction to rock climbing was mentioned, and in this chapter the basic skills of moving on rock faces are covered without discussing the use of ropes and other equipment.

The correct use of the feet and the development of good balance are the fundamental skills of rock climbing. These are best practised before an actual rock climb is attempted, and this physical and mental rehearsal can be a big help when the problems of rope handling and exposure to height are added to the basic problem of ascending the rock face.

On rocky paths or stream crossings, boulder hopping is a good way of improving balance and the co-ordination of eye and foot. It is possible to experiment with the use of different angles of friction and varied surfaces for the feet and to develop easy movement on rough ground.

However, it is in *bouldering* that many of the basic techniques of climbing can best be learned.

WHERE TO PRACTISE

Practice boulders (1) generally are rocks less than 15 feet high with grassy landings on to which it is possible to jump back down safely. Boulders situated below crags on which you intend to climb later often give similar characteristics of holds and moves and so this specific practice is of extra value.

As well as natural blocks, it is often possible to practise movements on the walls of old buildings (well built, ask permission!) and on old bridges although often this involves only a rather limited form of technique.

Finally, climbing walls (2) are springing up in sports halls and schools all over Britain, where it is possible for climbers to practise safely and develop skills and strength. Unfortunately, many of these are unsuitable for the nervous beginner and better practice of basic movement sometimes can be had in a conventional gymnasium.

WHAT TO WEAR

Clothing for rock climbing needs to be similar to that worn for hill walking, but allowing also for the slowness of rock climbing and the difficulty of retreat should the weather change. It should offer protection against wind, cold and rain; be light and roomy so that a full range of body movements is possible and be varied enough to cope with the wide range of conditions which may be met during a climb. Fingerless mitts are of

1. A typical boulder problem with a quite difficult crack.

2. A good example of an artificial climbing wall at Glenmore Lodge.

value for the hands whilst a variety of sweaters, windproof anoraks and waterproofs are used regularly. Many rock climbers wear jeans rather than breeches, although they tend to restrict movement and are useless when wet. However, for initial boulder sessions near the valley or on outcrops in the plains, little specialised clothing is required.

On the feet, for any real climbing in mountains, vibram-soled boots (3), preferably with a strengthened sole are good for most conditions. They should have narrow welts, fit close and have a pointed rather than a square toe. Gym shoes, basketball boots and special lightweight rubbers (4) for rock climbing are good for bouldering and for pure rock climbing, but they are very slippery in the wet and on grass and give very little ankle support. Kletterschuhe (5), which lie between the two, are not quite as good specifically as either of the other forms but they avoid some of the disadvantages.

3. A vibram-soled   4. Light-weight rubbers.   5. Kletterschuhe.
boot.

WHAT TO PRACTISE

The most important thing to do on boulders is to experiment. Whilst observation of the movements of others is helpful, most beginners are not born with an eye for isolating the components of a skilled climber's moves and so it is better to experiment with various positions of the body, hands and feet than blindly to follow the advice of others of different experience, physique and mental outlook.

Your first boulder climb should be something you can almost walk up without using the hands (6). Notice how the slightest change in the shape of the slab (slabs are rocks from 30°–60° steep) gives friction for the feet and that an apparently flat slab on closer examination has many variations of angle and form within it. Go up, down and across this rock until full foot confidence is developed, then experiment with various stances. Do the feet grip better with the heels low or on tip toe? Is it better to put the toe of the boot or the side of the boot on the hold?

Gradually go on to steeper slabs needing more than a simple staircase technique, and finally try a few walls (up to 90°) and an overhang. Practise jumping off before you fall off.

During this period of bouldering experimentation, it is worth practising controlled descent as well as climbing. Repetition refines technique and improves the quality of movement. From this practice, certain fundamentals should be discovered (24).

6. Young people scrambling on a very easy slab.

a. The importance of balance On any face up to 80° the weight can be kept over the feet and the hands used just to stay in balance. Conditioned games on boulder problems (for example, using one hand only) help to reinforce this.

b. Placing of feet Small steps involving accurate use of little footholds make movement smoother and less tiring. Well placed feet will stand on very small holds. Try banning large footholds on a practice problem.

c. Angle of boot sole Different types of footwear require different techniques. Generally speaking boots work best with the sole horizontal (3) and rubbers (4) with as much sole as possible in contact with the rock.

d. Body position Leaning in towards the rock tends to reduce the friction of the feet whilst hanging out tires the arms. Stand upright wherever possible.

e. Position of hands Reaching too high with the hands introduces two problems, reduction in the friction of the feet and rapid tiring of the arms. Use handholds at chest height or lower wherever possible.

f. Points of contact Although it is possible to hang from one hand or balance on one foot, you will find that it is better to aim for three secure points of contact with the rock and to move only one hand or foot at a time.

g. Loose holds Some holds are detached and it is best to test carefully any doubtful hold before trusting it.

h. Planning ahead The eyes are the most important part of a climber and right from the beginning you must train yourself to stand, often on small holds, and plan the next few steps instead of rushing up them. Plan a solution to the problem ahead then smoothly try the moves to see if they lead to another resting place. If this does not work, climb (reverse) back down to your starting position and think out another solution.

Fear of height and a fall inhibits movement and causes the climber to stand too close to the rock and to cling too firmly to his handholds. Right from the start you must strive to contain this fear and to believe that by adopting the correct posture and by using the best technique the danger of a fall is reduced considerably. It is this self control which is one of the biggest factors in a rock climber's make-up.

During early practice on boulders, as well as experimenting with the basic movements of rock climbing and using the correct clothing and footwear, a vocabulary of words describing rock features and movements and the basic characteristics of various rock types can be learned.

a. Features of a rock face

Glacis 0°–30°, *slab* 30°–75°, *wall* 75°–90°, *overhang* past vertical. A *crack* is any gap in the rock face from razor blade thickness up to one wide enough to just wriggle into sideways. Then it becomes a *chimney* until it is too wide to touch both sides, when it is called a *gully*. *Corners* are shaped like books opening up to a right angle. When acute angled they are often called *V chimneys* but as they open wider, they become *grooves*. A *rib* is a fairly blunt nose protruding from the rock whilst *arêtes* are much sharper edges. To a climber, a *ledge* means something he can stand on without use of the hands; a *niche* is a nook in a steep face, just man size, which usually is quite difficult to get out of. Caves are sometimes found in gullies and give hard problems unless a through route (often wet) is possible, otherwise it is necessary to climb the steep walls instead. Overhangs require extra use of the arms and if possible are 'turned' rather than climbed direct.

b. Types of rock

Most climbers think of igneous rocks such as granite and rhyolite as being the best to climb on. *Granite* generally is firm, in large rounded blocks with long cracks and few holds between them. *Gabbro* is very rough, coming in big walls and slabs. *Rhyolite*, one of the commonest climbing rocks in the Lake District and Snowdonia, varies from really firm good rock with spikes, cracks and slabs to looser grass covered rock which gets very greasy with lichen in wet weather. Of the sedimentary rocks which make up many of the outcrops both *sandstone* and *millstone grit* are usually found as short steep cliffs of rounded rock with rough cracks. Sandstone is softer so the holds become more rounded. Both tend to be overhanging in places due to generally horizontal beds. *Limestone* is smoother than those mentioned, sometimes with little pocket holds and thin cracks. Horizontal faults are usual, sometimes forming quite large overhangs. This rock gets much more slippery in the wet as does *mica schist* and other rocks of this type. Finally *quartz* can be found on many cliffs, sometimes as sharp crystals. It is generally considered unreliable due to its inherent brittleness.

SUMMARY
You will see that many things can and should be learned before actually tying on to a rope for a rock climb. The bigger the base of skill and knowledge both about the rock forms, mountains and weather and about the way rock problems are solved, the greater will be the pleasure and success found when bigger climbs are attempted and the more certain the possibility of success.

7. Students practising with top ropes on small practice rocks.

BASIC ROPE WORK

Having practised the basic movements of rock-climbing on small boulders, you arrive naturally at the stage of wanting to climb on bigger rocks, say 50 or 100 feet high. To do this you must be 'protected' from falling. This means that you will be tied to a rope which is properly held by an experienced companion, who himself is secured to the rock above you.

This chapter is concerned with the standard method of using a climbing rope between two people. Remember that climbers always move one at a time, with the static climber secured to the rock.

THE ROPE

It is important that you should use proper climbing rope. Usually it will be 120 feet long, or sometimes 150 feet for harder climbs.

Over the years, many materials have been tried for climbing ropes and each has advantages and disadvantages. Flax, manilla and Italian hemp all have now been discarded in favour of one of two types of rope, both made from nylon or some variety of it. These two types differ in their method of construction.

A *hawser-laid* rope is one in which fibres of nylon are twisted together to make strands and three strands are twisted together to make a traditional rope.

A *kernmantel* rope has a large number of parallel filaments running along its length protected by a braided sheath.

A rope constructed by either method is suitable for rock climbing provided it is of the correct breaking strain and that it stretches sufficiently when absorbing loads. Recommended specifications for single climbing ropes are either nylon hawser-laid No. 4 BS3104 ($1\frac{3}{4}$in circumference) with a minimum breaking strain of 4,200lb (1800Kg), or kernmantel 11mm to the UIAA standard with a minimum breaking strain of 5,000lb (2200Kg).

You will see from this that a new climbing rope should be able to hold a load of nearly two tons. With this load it will have stretched between one-third and two-fifths longer. These ropes made of nylon are light, strong, extensible, flexible, rot proof and washable. However, they cut fairly easily and so need checking regularly, and are adversely affected by being stored in sunlight. They melt at the fairly low temperature of 480°F (250°C). This low melting point is a serious disadvantage, because it can easily be reached by the fairly rapid friction of one piece of rope running over another, especially if the moving rope is loaded and the fixed one is in tension.

COILING AND UNCOILING THE ROPE

New ropes are bought either coiled in a fashionable way or on drums. Either way seems to introduce kinks into the rope and so first it is necessary to uncoil the rope into a pile and run it firmly through the hands, snaking it to send all the kinks off the end. It may be necessary to repeat this process. If you have space, kinks can be removed by stretching the rope out straight on the ground and twisting them off the end. Every time you use a rope, run it through before coiling, not only to dekink it but also to check for cuts or damage it may have sustained during a climb. Damaged ropes must be discarded.

There are many ways of coiling a rope, but some create unnecessary strains in the rope and the simplest will be described.

Take the rope in the left hand, palm upwards, allowing about a three foot end to hang down. With the right hand, make bandolier sized loops (not too big!) round the left hand either rolling the rope between thumb and fingers of the right hand so as to remove kinks or just laying it on the palm and tolerating the build up of kinks. When you reach the end leave three to four feet hanging there too. Fold the shorter end back to make a loop and then use the other end to whip about six turns tightly around the coils and this loop, working towards the loop. Tuck the whipping end through the loop and pull the other end to tighten it.

Uncoiling should be a complete reversal of this done one loop at a time. Always uncoil a rope completely before a climb, leaving both ends clear of the pile. Leaders tie to the top of the pile, seconds to the bottom.

HOW TO TIE ON TO THE ROPE
There are many methods of tying on, and all of them have some disadvantages. They can be classified into three main groups:
i. Tying direct to the end of the rope.
ii. Wearing some kind of belt with a sliding link and tying the rope to this link.
iii. Wearing a harness either round the hips or chest or both and attaching the rope to the front of this.

In Chapter x ('Harder climbing') and Chapter ix ('Artificial climbing') various methods of tying on will be considered but at this stage one simple system will be described – group ii, comprising belt, sliding shackle and karabiner.

8. One type of belt buckled correctly. Spare end should be tucked in.

9. Approved screw gate karabiner attached with figure of eight knot and double stopper knot.

a. *The belt* (8)

This is made of nylon webbing protected by a cotton sleeve to avoid any danger of melting by rope friction. It has a non-slip buckle and a shackle which slides freely. It will withstand strains of up to 4,500lb without the buckle slipping or the nylon breaking. However, care must be taken to do up the buckle correctly according to the maker's instructions.

b. *The link* (9)

A snap-link called a karabiner with a screw gate is used. It should have a tested strength of 5,000lb.

c. *The knot* (10, 11)

Climbers have used a variety of knots for this purpose, but the figure-of-eight knot tied off with some kind of stopper knot is recommended as adequate at this stage.

The fundamental aim of this or any other system of using the rope to join two climbers is that nowhere in the chain linking them is there a weaker link than the knot in the rope. Only belts, karabiners and ropes of guaranteed strength should be used.

10. Figure of eight knot.

11. Figure of eight knot with a stopper knot.

On small crags up to one hundred feet high, it is possible for one climber to walk round to the top and then to drop the rope down to his companion (see Chapter VIII, 'Rope throwing'). Both must attach themselves to the rope in the recommended way and both now should wear crash helmets (climbing helmets of an approved British Standard). Before the man on the ground (the second) starts to climb, the one at the top (the leader) must 'belay', that is, tie himself to something very secure, an anchor, and then take in and hold the rope in such a way as to keep it tight between himself and the second, even if the second were to let go of the rock. So as leader you have three steps to make – *a.* selecting your anchor, *b.* belaying yourself to it and finally *c.* taking in and holding the rope to your second. If *a.* or *b.* are done badly, then if a fall occurs both climbers will land at the foot of the crag. If only *c.* is done wrongly, then the second could get hurt and the leader burn his hands. It is vital on early top roping practice for both climbers to check the belaying system.

a. Selecting the anchor
Climbers belay to many things. On one outcrop it is possible to park a Land Rover parallel to the cliff top, leave it in gear with the hand brake on and then for the leader to use this as his anchor. Generally however, the leader has a choice of five different types of anchor.

1. Spike or flake (12) This is the most common form of anchor. If possible the spike should be located above shoulder height and it must be big enough for the rope placed over it not to roll or be lifted off. It should be given three tests. First examine it by *sight* to be sure that it is a solid part of the rock face and not a detached block or boulder, however large, lying on the ground or ledge. Secondly bang it with the heel of the hand. It should not *sound* hollow. Finally *feel* its security with a gradually increasing heave in the direction of possible strain, first making sure that if it comes away, you don't go with it! Spikes, apparently firm, have come away after years of use, so always make these tests as rigorous as possible. Never use dubious belays.

12. Full weight belay slip over fine spike. Screwgate of karabiner away from the rock.

2. Natural threads This is the best type of anchor, for it will take a pull in every direction. It is formed when two rocks are touching, by putting a loop or sling round the point of contact. In certain types of rock there is actually a hole through which the rope or a sling can be threaded.

3. Natural chockstones (13) Stones well jammed into a crack can make quite good belay anchors provided you are sure that they cannot be pulled out of the crack.

4. Trees The rope or a sling can be threaded round a tree provided the tree is strong enough, alive and well rooted. On

13. Chockstone thread. Tape slings unsuitable for this type of anchor.

all but the strongest trees, the sling is best placed as low as possible to lessen leverage on the trunk. This principle applies equally to flakes of course.

5. Manufactured chockstones and pitons The use of these will be discussed in Chapter v ('Protecting the Leader') and Chapter ix ('Artificial climbing').

Whatever choice of belay you make, as a general rule it is best to have at least two anchor points wherever possible. These should be on entirely separate areas of rock so that if one fails, the other will still be independently secure.

b. Belaying

As in most aspects of rope work, there are many ways of attaching yourself to the anchor point. However, one system is fairly standard with British climbers and this will be described. Although it is possible to use the rope itself for belaying, if the belay is not too big it is better to use a separate sling of rope or loop of tape of similar strength to the rope, with a 5,000lb screwgate karabiner, placed over the belay or through the thread (14). Tape loops are usually best over rounded spikes. Rope slings (tied or spliced), if necessary protected with leather sleeves, are better around chockstones and over sharp flakes.

Having placed the sling round the anchor, next you must select your stance. If the anchor point is high, then it is possible to stand with feet well braced on a firm flat area of the ledge in direct line between anchor point and the direction of pull should your second fall. Alternatively, with a low anchor, or a stance near the edge, it may be preferable to sit, again with the feet braced.

The method of tying to the anchor can be seen in photographs 15–17. Clip the rope from your waist through the screw gate karabiner on the sling, and screw up the karabiner.

14. Belay sling clipped directly into the belt. No adjustment possible.

15. Belaying i: Rope clipped in, karabiner screwed up with belayer stepping towards the anchor.

16. Belaying ii: Large loop pushed through waist karabiner.

17. Belaying iii: Figure of eight knot tied with a bight.

18. Belaying iv: Knot tightened, spare bight clipped into a second anchor point and rope held round waist and wrist.

Next make a two foot loop (a bight) in the rope coming back to you. Push this loop through your waist karabiner and tie a figure-of-eight knot back round the bight. In order to avoid slack rope in the belay, you should take one step towards the anchor while tying the knot. When tied, tighten the knot by pulling each strand firmly. There should be a loop of at least one foot hanging free.

19. Taking in i: Both ropes held in 'active' hand.

20. Taking in ii: Inactive hand moves back.

When using two belay points it is possible to repeat the full process into the second sling and karabiner; however, this uses a lot of rope and sometimes it may be possible to clip the spare loop formed into the second anchor (18). In this situation, both belays must be of equal tension.

Finally turn to face the possible direction of pull sliding the shackle and karabiner around your belt.

21. Taking in iii: Both hands take in.

c. Holding the second

Although there are many ways of holding a fall, some using special knots or mechanical devices, the standard method still uses the leader's hands and body as an indirect belay between the second and the anchor. In this way some of the load can be absorbed by the leader's legs and body and so less strain is put onto the anchor. You take the rope in, hand over hand, until it is tight to the second, then place it over your head and round your waist above your belt (18). Finally take a twist around the wrist furthest from the second on the 'dead' or inactive rope. The other hand, holding the 'live' or active rope, feels the tension and so can take in the rope and keep it taut to the second. It is rather like playing a fish, taking in as he moves up or paying out a little if he steps down again. Both hands move to take in, then the active hand goes forwards to hold both ropes and finally the inactive hand moves back (19–21). It is worth practising this action with another climber, paying the rope back and forth across a room. It is very important to ensure that there are no slack loops of rope anywhere between the second's waist and the leader's dead hand. Beginners particularly tend to let a loop build up behind their backs if the climber moves too quickly.

You will see from the photographs that the person handling the rope must brace forward the 'live' leg and wear gloves to protect the hands. Long leather gloves are best and the sleeve should be rolled down on the inactive wrist as extra protection.

On bigger climbs a complete set of calls should be used to communicate between the two climbers, but at this stage it is sufficient for you to tell the second to climb once all the rope is in and held ('Climb when ready') and the second to warn you as he prepares to leave the ground ('Climbing now') and then to wait while you make a complete check of your system. Always make this check. Do it in a logical order.

1. *The Anchor* Are you sure it is perfect? Will it take a load of nearly two tons like all the other links in the chain? (A loaded family car weighs $1\frac{1}{2}$ tons!)

2. *The belay loop and karabiner* Is it of the correct strength? Does it rest on any sharp edges? (These should be padded or rounded off.) Is the karabiner of the correct strength with a

22. Practice on the Plas y Brenin weight-drop machine.

screwgate screwed up? Is the screwgate away from the rock so that it cannot work loose under movement?

3. The belay Is the belay tight between you and the anchor? Are you well stanced so that a sudden jerk cannot pull you off balance? Are you in the best position to help and communicate with your second? Is your knot tight and correctly tied with a sufficient loop through it? Is your belt done up correctly and your screw gate screwed up?

4. Rope holding Are you wearing gloves? Is the twist around the correct wrist and the rope round your waist above your belt?

After all these checks, in fact the work of a few seconds, you have the final word, 'OK' and the second can then start to climb. Three other calls are worth using at this stage, 'Tight!' if the second is in difficulty or the rope is becoming rather loose between you, 'Slack!' if the rope is too tight to the second, and 'Below!' if a stone is dislodged or if the rope end is to be thrown down from the top of the crag.

It is good practice for the second to climb up two or three feet above the ground and then to jump off after first warning the leader. This type of practice can be extended by using sacks of sand or car tyres, or by using a weight-drop machine (22) similar to the one at the National Mountaineering Centre in North Wales.

SUMMARY
It can be seen that using a rope well can keep climbers quite safe, especially the second, but because of the complexities of belts, karabiners, knots, belays and rope holding, errors in rope work can increase the risk of injury to both climbers. *Always double-check rope work.*

BIGGER CLIMBS

In Chapter III we suggested that on small crags a climber could walk round to the top, make a belay and then drop a rope so that his companion could climb in safety. We now progress to bigger climbs, where this is not possible.

Bigger climbs are usually ascended in stages, with a stance at the top of each stage. These stages can vary between 20 and 150 feet, but each one is always called a 'pitch'.

The fundamental idea of the use of the rope on multi-pitch climbs is that at all times each climber is either securely belayed to an anchor or is protected by his companion holding the rope in a recognised fashion. Two climbers climbing a two pitch climb of say 200 feet would proceed as follows. The leader climbs up the first pitch of 100 feet whilst the second pays out the rope around his waist and dead wrist. If the ground below the rockface is steep, then the second will belay himself to an anchor. This habit is quite a good one for beginners. Not only does it give belaying practice in a safe place, but also it stops the second from stumbling around and plucking on the leader's rope while he is climbing.

In the next chapter, protecting a leader's slip is discussed but at this stage it is sufficient to adopt the old idea that leaders should not fall.

After 100 feet the leader reaches a ledge, the stance, and finds a sound anchor. He belays himself (23) and then informs his second using the conventional phrase 'Taking in'. This call means, to the second, that the leader is secured and safe and so he can stop holding the rope around his body and wrist. However, he should not just drop the rope, but having lifted it over his head, he should feed it up to the leader,

23. Leader on stance belaying. Second still belayed and holding leader's rope.

removing tangles. The leader can take in the rope hand over hand, for both climbers are safe, and pile it tidily on the stance beside him. Once all the slack rope has been taken in, the second (still belayed) shouts 'That's me'. Now it is the leader's turn to lift the rope over his head, and hold it around his body and wrist. He has put his gloves on and shouts 'Climb when ready'. The second removes his gloves, unties his belay knot (beginners sometimes undo their waist tying-on knot instead) and unclips from and collects the belay sling. The leader, if sensitive, will feel the spare rope freed from the belay system, and will take this in. The second shouts 'Climbing now' and after the usual rapid check of his belay system, the leader has the last word, 'OK'.

When the second reaches the stance, the leader should give him a little slack rope so that the second can belay himself whilst still held in safety by the leader. Only then may the leader lift the rope over his head and both climbers relax in comfortable security on the stance. On big stances, these precautions seem affected but as harder climbs are attempted, stances get smaller and more precarious and the need for good habits at the change-over becomes obvious.

Before the leader starts to climb the second pitch, the second must once again protect him. Then the leader can untie his belay knot, unclip from the anchor sling and karabiner, remember to screw up again the gate on this karabiner and continue. Now the second's role becomes more valuable, for if the leader falls on this pitch, the second may arrest his fall before he hits the ground.

The forces involved in a leader's fall are great (24) whereas a second falling can exert only a little over his own weight (a static load). A leader falling from 20 feet above his second will drop 40 feet before the rope goes tight and will have a dynamic force of many times his own weight. However, climbing ropes are quite elastic and so the full load is not felt suddenly but is absorbed, to a degree, by the rope. If the second does not snatch at the rope but slowly increases the wrist twist and also crosses his arms to increase the friction around his body, it is possible in theory, that he too may aid a gradual deceleration rather than try to cause a sudden stop. Certainly, within reason, this deceleration of a falling leader,

24. Leader well above second on quite steep rock. Many of the basic fundamentals of staircase techniques are demonstrated including balance, footwork, body position, use of eyes and three-point contact. A fall here would put considerable loads on the second.

by rope stretch and by some rope running, keeps loads low on the weaker parts of the system, namely the second's waist and legs, second's anchor and the leader's body. Once again, practice with a sack of sand and a weight-drop machine can be very valuable and indeed, surprising.

Finally the leader, not having fallen, reaches the top of the cliff, finds his anchor, belays, and after the usual calls, brings up his second in the top-roping manner.

This procedure of climbing in pitches with both climbers either belayed or held at all times can be extended for any number of pitches. A quicker way of proceeding is possible if both climbers are of the same standard of ability. This involves 'leading through' – that is leading alternate pitches so that no change over of belay is needed.

So far we have talked of two climbers in a team, but sometimes a party of three climbers go on a climb together. On other occasions, the number in one party is even larger. In this situation the leader climbs as usual up the first pitch and brings up his second. Now, either he can continue up the next pitch protected by the second or wait whilst his second brings up the third member of the group or bring up the third person himself. If his second is on his first or second climb then perhaps it is better to adopt the third course, while on small stances he must take the first alternative. Usually, however, it is best for him to wait whilst the third climber joins them, being brought up by the second, staying belayed himself in the meantime. On the next pitch whilst the second climbs, the third should protect him, not only for rope work practice but also in case the leader's belay fails.

Piling the rope on the stance as it is taken in is fairly uncomplicated in parties of just two climbers. The leader only has to remember that the pile of rope is upside down, that is, his rope runs from the bottom of the pile and not the top. If really careful, he will run it through before starting on the next pitch. However, with groups of three or four, each rope needs to be separately piled and each climber needs to be placed on the stance in the same order as on the rope if tangles are to be avoided. If a tangle does form in the rope, it is not wise to unrope during a climb and retie on. All tangles and knots should come out with careful unravelling.

GUIDE BOOKS

Climbing guide books have been written for almost every rock face in Britain, and are being revised continually. A good guide book will give a lot of information about an area and it is always worth reading it carefully from cover to cover before climbing there. Usually guide books have pictures or diagrams of crags and so routes can be identified as a cliff is approached. They tell you the easiest way to walk to the face and the simplest way to return to the bottom after completing the climb. The text gives the overall length of a climb, general comment on its type and difficulties and finally a pitch by pitch description with details of belays and stances. They describe the techniques needed, and often they indicate where the hardest part (the crux) lies on the climb. Routes are named by the first climbers to ascend them although certain notable challenges were named by earlier climbers who had failed to climb them. After doing a first ascent, the leader will send in details together with the proposed name to one of the senior climbing clubs which has made itself responsible for that particular area. Also, he will include his estimation of the standard of difficulty of the climb. These details, and particularly the standard, are usually checked before they are published in a guide book.

STANDARDS

Climbs are given some form of comparative grading in the guide book. These gradings are the opinions of the guide book writer in conjunction with the views of his friends etc. They are intended to serve as a rough indication of the difficulty of the route in favourable conditions and usually refer to the hardest pitch of the climb. In Britain most climbs are given a verbal grade and fit into one of the following categories.

Easy — scramble where a rope is needed.

Moderate (Mod) — easy angled rock which has big hand holds and good stances.

Difficult (Diff) — steeper but still having good holds. Often the holds on popular difficult climbs have been very worn by nailed boots, making them quite hard.

Very Difficult
(*V Diff*)
— longer pitches, smaller holds needing more than the usual staircase technique. Often seem to be strenuous.

Severe
— steep open climbs needing experience.

Very Severe (*VS*)
— hard climbs needing lightweight footwear, strength and skill. Sometimes well nigh impossible in poor weather conditions.

Hard Very Severe
(*Hard VS*)
— a sub-division for routes too hard to be called VS yet not desperate enough to be given the highest grading.

Extremely Severe
(*XS*)
— the hardest climbs at present.

WEATHER

On outcrops it is unusual for weather to overtake a climber during a route, but on multi-pitch climbs, which are usually found on mountains anyway, objective dangers of this sort must always be considered. Rain makes rocks slippery both for the feet and the hands, whilst snow and ice can make even quite easy climbs virtually impossible. A strong wind makes balance more precarious and also tangles and snags ropes and makes communication much more difficult. Not only is the present weather important, but some knowledge of previous weather helps a climber to decide how wet rocks will be and how much frost has loosened holds. The effect of weather on crags is influenced by the direction they face and their height above sea level. In winter, weather is not the only objective danger, for climbers must be aware also of the shortness of the day and so start early for big climbs.

Once a climber realises the vital importance of weather in mountains he can use his knowledge to snatch climbs at times when, apparently, conditions are not good for climbing.

SUMMARY

It can be seen that the problems and dangers increase quite considerably on bigger multi-pitch climbs. Even after the climb, two extra areas of danger still exist. These arise from taking off the rope too early at the top of a crag and carelessness on descents. Never relax until you are back on the road. However, with careful thought and planning these extra hazards can be contained and the greater rewards of full mountain days truly enjoyed.

25. The leader has placed a stopper running belay fifteen feet above his second and continues in comparative safety.

5 PROTECTING THE LEADER

In Chapter IV it was assumed that the leader should not fall – and yet leaders do fall and survive. Even the most careful leader can have an apparently sound hold break off or be dislodged himself by a falling stone or even, in these days of crowded crags, by a falling climber. Sometimes leaders lose the route and get on to rock too hard for them, or just over-estimate their own skill and form on the day and so run out of holds or strength. Some falls have been attributed to a leader's blind faith in a guide book writer's estimate of a climb's difficulty. Climbs do change, holds and trees fall off and alter the characteristics of a route and so the leader should re-member that a guide book can only give an indication of the standard of the climb. The sport of rock climbing involves calculated risks and yet modern equipment has made it possible to stay fairly safe on most routes whatever their standard. The skill of protection is an art and has made many of the hardest modern climbs possible.

The basic idea involves the use of *running belays*. At the start of this century, leaders simply hooked their rope behind flakes or spikes of rock in passing so that if they fell, a pulley system was created. Often the rope cut through or jammed or broke off the flake but sometimes this crude running belay worked. On some hard chimney pitches, the leader would untie from the end of the rope, thread it behind a chockstone and then retie and continue. Stories are told of frightened seconds trying to climb through the narrow hole after the rope, not realising what the leader had done.

Later a refinement of these crude runners was introduced. Lengths of the rope were cut off when needed and knotted through threads or into slings round spikes, the climbing rope being threaded through the loop thus formed. However, with the invention of the karabiner, made up slings appeared on the market and the first modern runners were in use.

Nowadays, leaders can 'stitch' their rope to the cliff face, clipping it to a great variety of running belays. In fact, a really cautious (sensible? cowardly?) leader can place a running belay above himself, clip the rope through it and actually climb a few hard moves on a type of top rope.

BASIC THEORY

Fundamentally, it seems wise to try to place a very good running belay on a pitch as soon as possible (25). If the rope is clipped through a karabiner on a strong (4,000lb) sling placed over a firm spike, a *stopper runner* is formed. Any fall now will exert an upwards pull on the second. A fall from twenty feet above the second without runners will result in a forty feet drop before the rope tightens and a very heavy downward load would be put on the second. Only twenty feet of rope is available to absorb the fall and the leader could hit the stance or the rocks below it. With a stopper runner at ten feet, only a twenty feet fall is possible, the force on the second is upward and so is partly counteracted by his own weight. The rope available to stretch is still twenty feet and some energy is absorbed also by friction in the running karabiner and sling.

Ideally leaders, particularly those climbing near their known limit, should aim for a stopper runner as soon as possible and then one every twenty feet. Others of varied strengths may be placed between these and at the crux.

The using of runners introduces a minor problem for the second. Normally main belays are selected so as to take a downward pull; however, with a stopper runner above him a second, particularly if he be a lightweight, may be in danger of being lifted bodily off his stance when counter balancing a leader's fall (26). Hence it is good practice to have a belay which will take strains in all directions (a natural thread or a piton) or to place a second belay designed to take an upward pull for a leader using running belays.

Acting as a second, particularly to a leader using suspect

runners, introduces other important finesses. When the leader brings up a second it is obvious in which way he must face. He has his back to the anchor point so the rope runs behind his waist and across his belt. However, when paying out to a leader, it is easy for the second to make the mistake of facing his belay so that, if the leader falls, the strain comes behind him down the cliff and the rope is wrenched from his hands. Hence it is vital that the second stands facing outwards when paying out the rope to his leader. If the leader is above and to his right as he faces out, he must pay out the live rope using the right hand and use the left hand and wrist-twist to control the dead rope. If the leader passes above him and wishes to continue on his left then either he must ask the leader to stand

26. Light second belayed and standing correctly prepared for an upward pull once the running belay is reached.
Right 27. An attentive unbelayed second on the ground.

still while he changes over the rope (a dicey business) or he can make a half turn in that direction keeping the rope and live hand in front of him.

The fundamental aim always must be that, in the event of a runner-less fall, as the second takes the load, the rope always must be across his back above the belay chain. Seconds continually should expect a leader to fall and place themselves accordingly.

This procedure appears to be complicated by the presence of dubious runners. However, if the runner does not break, the pull can be held without too much trouble so the second must expect the runner to fail when deciding his position. Good seconds pay complete attention to all the leader's actions (27). It tires the neck to watch the leader throughout each pitch but this constant observation, coupled with sensitive holding of the rope, can help the leader considerably and give the second immediate warning of a leader fall.

Another skill which a second needs to develop is the ability to feed quickly a few feet of rope to the leader when required. For example, if the leader reaches a steep crux, he will stand for some time studying it and then suddenly he will 'go for the move' making three or four smooth, rapid moves to reach the next resting place. In teams where the rapport between a leader and second is great, the second can help the leader up this section by virtually pushing the rope up as he moves.

There is another occasion when a sensitive second can be extremely valuable is at the 'clipping in to runners' stage. The leader places a high runner. He is tired and wants to get his rope through it as quickly as possible. If the second is half asleep, then the ensuing battle for slack rope could have the leader off, so a good leader will communicate by saying 'Runner on, slack'. The ever-ready second, having watched the runner being placed, already will be pushing up the extra few feet of rope. If his leader looks in a really bad way, the second will take in any slack and be ready for the load as soon as he hears the click of the karabiner and the leader's 'Thank God'.

Good seconds are rare and worth their weight in gold – they rarely need to buy their own drinks!

a. Sling runners Rope loops of various lengths, thicknesses and strengths from 5,000lb (also usable for belays) down to 500lb (useless for any fall over one foot) can be carried to place over spikes and to thread through holes or around chockstones.

b. Tape runners Various lengths, widths and types of tape give strong runners to edge down narrow cracks behind flakes and to place over rounded bulges.

c. Inserted chockstones In the 1950's, climbers often carried in their pockets a variety of rounded pebbles to place in cracks. This practice now has ended with the production of artificial chocks.

d. Jammed knots Another discarded idea was to tie knots in slings and to jam these in cracks.

e. Jammed nuts Chockstones were superseded by the idea of threading industrial nuts, with their threads drilled out, on to appropriately-sized lengths of rope or line, and jamming these nuts into cracks.

f. Artificial chockstones (28–31) Today a wide range of alloy, and even plastic chockstones are manufactured either already

28. Artificial chocks. Assorted sizes and shapes on wire loops.

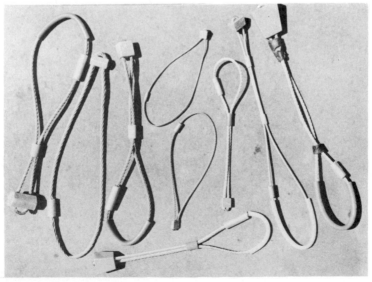

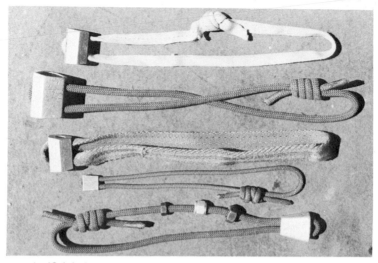

29. Artificial chocks. Assorted sizes and shapes on tape and rope loops

30. A wedge-shaped chock ideally placed in the narrowing of a crack. Avoid resting chocks on rugosities.
Right 31. Two hexagonal chocks placed in different directions.

threaded onto wire slings of known breaking strength or drilled out ready for rope, line or tape to be threaded through them. When threading your own it is pointless to have too long a sling in the chock, about 8in from chock to karabiner seems reasonable.

g. *Pitons, etc* (See Chapter ix, 'Artificial climbing').

Many of the above runners require a sling to be formed. Only two knots need to be used – for rope slings a double fisherman's knot (32) and for tape slings a tape knot (33).

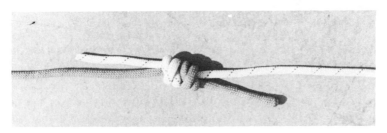

32. Double fisherman's knot.

33. Tape knot (loose).

THE STRENGTH OF RUNNING BELAYS

Although ideally runners should be as strong as any link in the climber's chain, in fact it is not often possible to place stoppers. Any runner, however weak, can have some value if only the climber understands its limitations. A minimum usable strength would be something very low indeed, for not only can a runner help to arrest a fall but it can also act as a pulley from which a tired or failing leader can retreat with a tight top rope from his second. Also, although a runner may break under the force of a leader's fall, it will have absorbed some of his energy and his fall may restart at a lower point.

One problem with running belays is that although it is possible to know what range of force a runner will take, and so to equip it with a karabiner of similar strength, it is not possible to know how strong the flake is on which it rests, or how much force will tear the rock away from the walls of the crack in which it is jammed. Experience and common sense should give basic guide lines, and provided estimates are on the safe side, and seconds warned to let some rope run for falls on doubtful or low strength runners, even these can and have averted serious leader falls.

CARRYING RUNNERS

It is useless to have a wide selection of runners and the skill to place them if they are carried in such a way as to be unavailable when most needed. Most climbers have their own ideas on this subject but certain basic needs can be considered when formulating your own method.

Long, strong rope slings usually are needed only on stances or large holds, so they can be put on first, doubled (if nine feet long) and worn bandolier fashion. Knots should be placed under the arm to prevent snagging on other slings. Some climbers clip these slings round as though using the shoulder and body as a chock and, to remove the sling, they unclip the karabiner from the back strand and pull it through. One or two of these very strong slings need to be equipped with strong, screwgate karabiners. On any doubled sling it is vital to clip the karabiner into both strands so that, if a slip occurs, one loop is less likely to hook onto a spike so resulting in the other loop tightening and strangling the climber.

Shorter line and tape slings are usually put over the head with knots at the bottom of the necklace so formed. Put them on one at a time. Longest first, shortest last is a standard rule unless it is possible to see the first spike runner and so to have the appropriate sling available.

Artificial chocks are best carried one to a karabiner. Then they can hang either from a single bandolier sling, or be attached in groups of four to spare shackles on the belt (34) or to a spare alloy karabiner clipped to the belt. In any case, it is

34. Leader carrying strong bandolier slings and assorted chocks on a spare shackle on her belt.

wise to 'rack' chocks in order of type and size so that the correct one can be found easily. Both with chocks and line slings, karabiners should be alloy with easily opening gates. In theory, the weaker the sling the lighter the karabiner needed. However, in the confusion of a hard route, this could mean that some strong slings get weak karabiners on them in error, so a minimum strength of 1800Kg (4,000lb) is recommended with some stronger karabiners for stoppers.

Finally, as well as all this gear draped around you, it is worth having a short length of thin line (4 or 5mm) in your pocket, unknotted, to thread through very fine holes and cracks.

The problem these days is not to find protection but to select from the variety of gear available the correct type and the right number for any particular climb. It is worth studying the guide book, looking at the rockface itself and assessing the various merits of your runners for any particular route. On slabs, tapes and small chocks may be much more use than big hexagonal chocks and full weight slings; on steep wide cracks

35. Meshach i: Badly placed **runners** on this very severe climb make leader movement almost impossible. Note particularly the acute bends in the rope at the first, second and last runner.
Right 36. Meshach ii: Extending some, tying all others and omitting the last runner considerably reduces rope drag.

the opposite may be true. There will be a maximum that a normal climber can carry. Two long rope slings and one long tape sling, bandolier fashion (all the same way!) should be ample. Six to ten assorted tape and line slings, and between six and sixteen assorted chocks on wire and rope or tape would seem to offer sufficient choice for most routes up to Hard VS.

PLACING OF RUNNERS
Not only must the leader use his runners correctly (30, 31), he must also remember that each time the climbing rope passes through a karabiner, friction results, particularly if the karabiner causes the rope to bend through an angle. A rope threaded through half-a-dozen runners in a zig-zag fashion will be almost immovable (35) and so the climber must extend many of his shortest wire chocks so that the line of the rope is as near straight as possible (36). Similarly, although it

is often possible to put a doubled sling on a spike, so strengthening the runner and shortening the fall, it may be best, if this causes a sharp bend in the rope, to have it single instead. A wire chockstone sometimes will lift out with rope friction as the climber continues unless it is 'tied off'. This means clipping a short tape or rope sling to it with an extra karabiner. This tying off or extending of runners is also necessary when a leader passes an overhang or puts a runner near a corner.

So far runners have been discussed only with regard to the leader, but often a runner can be placed to protect the second also, particularly on traverses and diagonal pitches where an unprotected second fall could result in a swing onto blank rock. Two classic cases should be considered. In the first, the leader climbs vertically above his second, fixes a runner and then traverses to a stance (38). This is good protection for both climbers. However, if the leader first traverses, then places his runner and climbs vertically to a stance, this runner is only good for him, for the second faces a nasty

37. Meshach iii: Double rope gives two nearly parallel lines through all runners with ample protection and little drag.
Right 38. Runner used to protect both leader and second.

pendulum if he falls off the first few steps from his stance. In this case, the leader either should protect the second with another rope direct from leader to second, or the runner should be of the type which will lift off once the leader is up.

Whenever the leader clips the rope into a runner he should ensure that the rope will not catch in his legs on its way to the runner (39) which would result in his being upended should he fall. Leaders in corners with the rope attached behind their backs have fallen outside the rope to a runner in the corner, and have been turned completely over to hit the backs of their heads against the rock. No standard rule is possible but it is always useful to imagine what would happen to the rope in a fall. Many of these runner problems cease once the leader starts to use double rope on harder routes (37) (Chapter x).

COLLECTING RUNNERS

As the second climbs he must collect runners, trying to rack them in a similar way to the leader so that once on the stance

39. A leader, well loaded with gear, with one rope (clipped in) absolutely clear of his legs. If the lower rope was still between his legs, a fall would up-end him.

he can hand them over quickly and efficiently. This passing over of runners is sometimes forgotton by over-tense or very keen leaders. Short slings should be lifted off spikes and placed over the head, then unclipped from the rope; longer slings should be placed over the head singly, given a single twist to a figure-of-eight shape and then the second strand placed over the head and the karabiner clipped into both strands. In precarious positions chocks are best left clipped to the rope until they are removed from the rock. A long, knife-like ice piton makes an ideal lever for removing jammed chocks and could become part of a second's gear on harder routes.

OTHER RUNNER TRICKS

The leader will find that a wire hook made from a dry cleaner's coat hanger is very useful both for hooking slings through tight threads and for clearing out thin cracks to provide chock placements.

One recurrent problem is that runners on poor spikes roll or lift off. One solution is to weigh them with heavy karabiners, bunches of pitons or even a piton hammer. Other ideas are the use of chewing gum or even adhesive tape to hold them down! Certainly, a long sling runner on a small spike stands more chance of staying on than a short one. However, if a line sling is to be left on a small spike as an aid to descent or retreat, then a very short sling will flick off more easily than a long one.

SUMMARY

Running belays make leading safer but often skill and ingenuity are needed to find this protection. Initially it looks as though the main value of runners is in arresting falls. However, two other factors due to runners help to make leaders safe and more successful. The psychological value of a good runner is immense. Rock which seems steep and holdless while you are unprotected, leans back and sprouts jug handles once a stopper is placed. Similarly, good runners break up a pitch into a series of small pitches, each virtually a boulder climb with the runners offering places to which a leader can retreat and rest after a tentative attempt at a series of moves. It is by these factors, plus their value in aiding escapes, that runners help to avert leader accidents.

SPECIALISED TECHNIQUES

In Chapter II, the basic staircase technique was introduced involving purely natural movements. On harder climbs, unnatural movements are needed too. Many of these movements are given names which are referred to in guide books.

HANDHOLDS

A *jug handle* is a very good handhold, over which all the fingers can curl and from which a climber can hang out a little to improve foot friction. Care must be taken not to cling more firmly than is needed which would waste strength. If a jug handle is high above you, you should reach for it and move up, not reach and hang.

On smaller handholds, it is important to search out minor rugosities to improve the grip, whilst in small pockets it is worth trying various combinations of fingers to get maximum value.

With the smallest of handholds it may help to raise the knuckles so that the very ends of the fingers and the finger nails rest on the hold. When pulling up on both hands on small holds preparatory to reaching for a good high hold with one hand, it helps to sag down a little first and then to pull and reach in one movement.

However, using horizontal holds to hang from is not their sole use, for often it is possible to press down on a hold to assist upward progress, even if it is rounded. These *pressure holds*, using the heel of the hand, give stronger moves than pulling up, fingers do not get tired and once the arm is straight the elbow can be locked and the position held for some time. When a climber has to climb a blank wall to get onto a good

40. Mantelshelf i: Use the feet to gain height.

41. Mantelshelf ii: 'Deep breath'.

42. Mantelshelf iii: Press through and adjust.

43. Mantelshelf iv: Toe on edge.

flat ledge, this technique is used for both hands, and a *mantel-shelf* move results. In the sequence (40–43), the climber first grasps firmly the good holds on the ledge, looks for higher handholds but sees none, and so is committed to mantelshelf. Although now faced with an arm pull, she uses her feet on poor holds to get as high as possible, sags, and then flicks through to a straight arm pressure hold position. Here she may pause to adjust her hand position slightly and then step up with one foot onto the ledge, placing the foot as near the hands as possible. Balance is precarious and smooth, strong continual movement is necessary for this manoeuvre. In the past, it was considered very bad form to use a knee, but provided there is a handhold within reach, now there seems to be no valid objection.

Although horizontal handholds are most common, some-times the climber must use vertical edges and cracks. He can use these *side-pulls* (44) in two ways, either simply as an aid to balance in opposition perhaps to another similar hold or as a layback hold. In *laybacking*, the climber uses both hands on the same edge, and pushes with both feet in opposition. On the slab illustrated (45), this is not too strenuous, but on vertical or overhanging rocks, a layback can be found to be one of the most strenuous moves in climbing (46).

Every effort should be made to use any footholds that appear and to move in a rhythmic way, hand – hand – foot –

44. Small side-pull hold.

45. Simple layback on a slab.

46. Vertical layback – left foot about to move.

foot. Also, it is important not to get the hands too far from the feet, otherwise the feet will slip down.

Two other types of handholds are worth noting. Sometimes a flake points downwards or an overhang has cracks under it, in which case the hands can be used palm upwards in opposition to the feet on the *undercut hold* so formed. On steep rock this is quite tiring but at least the hands are kept low and the foot friction improved. Finally, some small noses of rock can be pinched between thumb and fingers and this *pinch-grip* (47) used to maintain balance or to aid a gentle move upwards.

47. Fingers jammed in a crack and thumb used to pinch grip the edge.

CLIMBING CRACKS AND CHIMNEYS

Vertical fissures in rockfaces range from hairline cracks to wide gullies but whatever size they are, they offer some means of progress to the climber. Those up to half an inch are only climbable artificially with pitons or jammed chocks but once a climber can get his fingers into a crack, it becomes of use as a hold. From this size up to six feet wide there is always some part of a climber's body which will jam into the gap.

Imagine you are climbing a pitch up a vertical, irregular crack 150 feet high which starts five feet above the ground and widens as it rises to finish nearly six feet across. At first only the tips of the fingers will go into the crack and you must search for minor variations in width and then twist the fingers to make them jam. In some places you can use the thumb as well in a pinch grip (47); in other places it may be better to jam the fingers, thumb downwards, to increase the twisting effect (48). Higher it may be possible also to *sprag* (49) with the thumb to increase the grip of the fingers. It is possible to pull up on finger jams alone but this is very strenuous and so you must search for small footholds.

48. Reversed finger jam with thumb sprag.

49. Thumb sprag in a crack too wide to finger jam.

50. A hand jam with thumb across the palm.

51. Jack Street resting using a hand jam and one foot hold.

You need to climb these early moves quickly and confidently to save strength so that after about ten feet you can reach a wider place where the whole hand will slot into the crack, a perfect *hand jam* (50). Once jammed it takes little strength to keep the hand there (51), but you must try to stand well out from the rock (hang from the jam) (52) to improve the footholds.

As the crack slowly widens, the width of the hand jammed must be increased. You do this by bringing the thumb across the palm so increasing the thickness of the hand. At this stage, if you are wearing rubbers (53), you may be able to wriggle the tip of your boot, on its side, into the crack and twist the boot to jam it as well. So far running belays have been easy to place (artificial chocks) but later it may be hard to find protection.

52. Dennis Grey hanging from a hand jam and a pocket hold.

53. Jack Street using a toe jam, and side-pulls for the hands.

Once conventional hand jams run out, you change to *fist jams*, placing the hand across the crack and then clenching the fist. This makes a kind of bone chockstone, and in fact many of the least tiring jams are created by jamming bones across the crack rather than using muscle strength. One snag you will have noticed on this jamming section of the pitch is that good jams hurt. If you are careless, or if the rock is very rough, you may lose a little skin.

After about twenty-five feet of climbing, you should be able to push the whole of your arm into the crack, pressing shoulder to elbow on one wall and the palm on the other and using the edge of the crack by your face for the other hand as a side pull. Now your foot will fit nicely in the crack and you feel fairly secure. Do not use more strength than you need at this stage.

As the crack widens, the slope of the forearm decreases and first the knee and then the thigh can be jammed until at forty feet the arm is braced across the crack. When jamming boots or knees, care must be taken to place them, remembering the twist needed so that they can be slid out again. Half-a-dozen climbers have had to be rescued due to jammed knees. This is quite a frightening experience. In every case the knee had slipped deeper into the crack than necessary and when bent, had stuck.

Once the crack becomes more than a foot wide, you can wriggle inside and it has become a chimney. One important decision must be made at this stage. Which way do you face? Ideally you should face the wall with most holds on it and turn your back on any smooth, overhanging walls. Tight chimneys are very strenuous and awkward and if holds exist on the outside, it is often more pleasant and elegant to stay on the face. Once inside, the secret is to stay cool and to search for the smallest rugosities both for the hands and for the feet. It is often possible to wriggle up a little and then rejam the body while you rest. Hands generally are of more use on downward pressure holds than for pulling on little finger cracks. Remember that in many chimneys the two walls are complementary, that is, if the wall facing you has a little overhang on it, the one behind you may have a little ledge on it. Now your boots may jam across the chimney horizontally. As it gets wider the knees, toes and palms rest on one wall, the back on the other. Later, one hand can push on each wall and the femur (thighbone) can wedge across the gap to give a solid support.

After about ninety feet, the chimney is wide enough to use *back and foot* technique (54), the classic way to climb chimneys. Either both feet are placed on one wall and both hands and the back on the other and they are moved alternately (*backing up*), or one foot and one hand may be used on one wall and the back, hand and foot on the other. Once again the use of bulges etc make this procedure much more secure.

Finally comes the most elegant and least strenuous part of all. The two walls are now over three feet apart and so you can *bridge* (55) up with one foot and one hand on each wall using every hold possible. Because you are pressing outwards, quite

54. Resting in a back and foot position in a shallow chimney.

55. Bridging and using hand jams.

poor holds are usable. Most of your weight should be on your feet and you can face into the depths of the chimney, if you wish to look for runners, or be bold and face outwards.

With twenty feet to go, the chimney is too wide to bridge and so you must climb either its walls or go to the rear where two corners and the back wall complete it. One of these corners is a V chimney and so you can continue up this, still bridging but using hand jams in the corner crack. Here you will find that the wider you bridge, the less you need to hang on with your hands – in fact, with good wide bridging a vertical corner can feel like a slab.

STEEP SLABS AND WALLS

No special technique exists for these problems other than combinations of those mentioned earlier. However, some variation in the basic staircase technique (24) does help on steep rock. Sometimes it is better to step up sideways on to the rock rather than lean out too far to let the knee through, and quite often it will help a climber with weak arms to get both feet up onto one hold before straightening up and reaching for higher handholds. Often steep areas of rock are traversed and this is not as hard a manoeuvre as it looks, for the body weight does not have to be raised on every move. *Hand traverses* are places for rapid, rhythmic movement. When using footholds on a traverse, a climber must choose between stepping through, that is taking one foot inside the other to reach the next hold, and changing feet on each hold either by an exciting hop or by putting one foot on top of the other and then slowly sliding out the lower foot. One good thing about traverses is that leader falls put a gradually increasing load on runners and seconds rather than the usual shock load.

DESCENDING

Chimneys and gullies can give easy descents but climbing down steep slabs and walls is quite difficult, although on all descents gravity is helping. The basic rule is to keep the hands low. On easy rock it is usual to face outwards and use pressure holds for the hands and backside friction as well. As the rock gets steeper, turn sideways so that at least one hand can use jug handles. On very steep rock, face in and lean well out in order to spot the route. Kick holds to check their firmness before swinging down onto them. Generally it is harder to descend than to ascend but protection from above is often possible. When in doubt, abseil as described in Chapter VIII

SUMMARY

One of the hardest tasks on vertical rock is to conserve strength. Obviously, good technique is much less tiring than bad technique but it is equally important for the good climber to recover his strength during a pitch. After a few hard moves, an excited leader will race up the next easier section and get involved in another hard part of the pitch. He would be much better advised to linger on this easier section, recouping his strength for the higher problem and also checking that he is still going the right way.

Boulders and climbing walls give opportunities to practise many of these specialised techniques, and of course personal fitness also will improve performance in this area of climbing.

STARTING TO LEAD

Many climbers start to lead quite early in their climbing career and either through ability, lots of luck, or lack of imagination survive their early mistakes and become safe climbers. However falls, sometimes fatal, or a loss of nerve and a giving up of the sport are all too frequent at this stage and so in recent years, teachers have made an effort to study this critical stage in a climber's development with some care. In the more paternal climbing clubs, a young climber is given the chance to lead, at a lower standard, after a season or so of seconding at higher standards and this is a good way to introduce this critical step. Today many young climbers do not join clubs and so other solutions are needed. The problem can be considered by looking at two areas. First by defining the skills a leader needs and then by examining various methods and practices which cover some of the skills each time so that it is possible gradually to build up to *sight leading* of multiple pitch climbs. Few aspirant leaders or teachers cover every practice described here yet each one can give great fun and some can usefully occupy wet or companionless days. Certainly the foundation so gained can lead to many happy days climbing rockfaces.

THE SKILLS
The five skills a leader needs are as follows:

A. Physical ability This is the fundamental skill of being able to climb rocks above the lowest standard with economy of effort, good smooth movement and balance. The leader needs sufficient extra strength to hang around placing protection as well as purely to climb the rocks. If you are unable to follow easily at Very Difficult standard, you would be ill advised to try to lead Difficult routes.

B. Intellectual skill This is the ability to recognise your climb with the aid of a guide book, to see the possible line and to evaluate the difficulty of each part of a pitch by just looking at it. Although you can climb at Difficult standard and you are trying a Difficult climb, if you wander from the correct route, the standard could quickly reach VS.

C. Rope work The leader is solely responsible for finding belays, for handling the rope and adequately safeguarding the second. He must decide the second's stance and position him correctly.

D. Protection Leaders need to select the correct set of gear for a route, to place sufficient protection and to understand its limitations.

E. Psychology The mental pressures on a leader are many and varied. He must learn to accept exposure, to take responsibility for a party and to develop self-control when things go wrong. He must be motivated to want to lead; for this, above all, is the main requirement of a leader.

THE METHODS
The following variations on the basic climbing theme give an aspirant leader the opportunity to break down the skills of leading and to practise them in a less total form. In each suggested practice, the skills involved, if practised to the full, are indicated by capital letters which refer to the previous paragraph. If only partially involved the skills are indicated by small letters.

It is not necessary to follow the exact order in which the practices are described, but generally ones later in the list do depend on skills acquired earlier. Some can be practised alone or with non-climbing friends, some need a friend of similar experience and some need the help of more expert climbers.

1. Following bigger climbs A c Climbing as an observant second on multi-pitch climbs gives many opportunities to watch your leader deal with problems and often to observe other leaders around you. Study particularly the placing of protection. Try to follow some longer climbs at Very Difficult or Severe standard before thinking of leading.

2. Top roping hard, one pitch climbs A   This purely physical practice should be taken to its logical conclusion, that is attempting problems of progressive difficulty on a top rope until you fall off. This will let you realise your physical limits. As a leader your limit may be much lower! Try not to take aid from the rope at this stage for this can give a false impression.

3. Belay practice C   This and the two following practices can be done alone or in bad weather. Wander around a boulder field trying to find belays, and then test them fully. Tie on to them and check the relative strengths of the links in the chain. Imagine pulls in various directions. Will the belay stand them? Visualise the worst possible train of events. Will you still be secure? Really spend a couple of hours thinking about belaying both as leader and second to the exclusion of all other climbing skills.

4. Runner practice (56) D   Select a good set of runners, hang them round you in a logical way and then go to the base of a small outcrop and within a limited area, try to place the runners securely on the rock. Clip a long spare sling to each one and test it with small loads, first standing then jumping in the sling. Try to estimate the size of dynamic load each one will take. Consider it not in terms of breaking force but by asking yourself the question 'How far above that runner do I need the next?' The answer could be anything from one to twenty feet. This is perhaps the most valuable practice of all. If you are with a friend, you can make it into a competition. Next go to your favourite boulder problems. Climb them unroped but this time place as many runners as possible up each one. Finally try to climb these problems artificially (see Chapter IX) using slings and chocks for aid.

5. Route spotting B   This game can bring added interest to a hill walking day. Go to the foot of a strange crag or outcrop and try to guess where the various routes go and to estimate

56. Pupil and instructor discuss the relative merits of various runners placed at the foot of a gritstone outcrop.

their standards. Then refer to the relevant guide book and check your estimates. This is also the way for a hard climber to spot new climbs, for knowledge of existing routes often inhibits ideas.

6. Following traverses A C e   Most crags and outcrops have girdle traverses right across the crag. As the second on these, you are not so well protected by the rope as on straight up routes and so become much more aware of the consequence of any errors.

7. Leading down A B C D   Going first down a climb involves all the skills of leading without the danger. With a better climber you can lead down a pitch, route finding, belaying, making decisions and most important of all, placing protection for your companion. Remember to place the runners below the hard moves not above them! Now your second can follow down checking the protection and advising you on its suitability. Initially, it is wise to practise this on routes your companion can solo down or both use top ropes.

8. Leading traverse pitches A B C D E   This introduces all the problems of leading except for the danger of long falls.

9. Leading through on easy pitches B C E   Often on a harder (V. Diff.) climb there is the occasional short easy pitch. If you lead this, the contrast to the difficulty of the other pitches will make it quite an easy lead. Also, it will give your leader a brief break.

10. Top rope runnering A B C D   For this you need a group of three aspirant leaders and two ropes. One of the group top ropes the second up a single pitch route. He places runners and clips the third man's rope through them. Finally number three climbs checking the runners then removing them.

11. Leading a prepared pitch (57) A C E   This practice could follow the previous one, but it is best if possible that a very experienced climber prepares the pitch. All necessary runners have been previously put in place and you lead the route clipping in as you reach them. This is a very important practice for, given good runners, it allows you to lead in comparative safety. Study the runners and occasionally place an extra one of your own. If you do this practice with a good teacher, gradually he will cut down the number of runners he places, expecting you to place your own runners at the more obvious spikes and threads.

12. Leading with prepared kit A C D E   On a fairly easy pitch, you are given the correct runners needed to protect it and a little information about where to place them. Then you are on your own.

13. Leading a followed climb A C D E   This time you follow a climb watching the leader's route finding and protection and then lead it. Repetition of routes and practices does help considerably to build up confidence. The more immediate the repetition, the easier the relead.

14. Sight leading one pitch climbs A B C D E   Now you are ready to select a route of the appropriate standard from your guide book and to lead it on sight. If you do not know what standard to choose you are not ready to lead! It may be a good idea to have someone with a top rope standing by. He should be

57. Expert instructor, solo, placing runners for aspirant leader.

belayed at the top of the route, with his rope uncoiled and a knot in the end with a karabiner clipped to it.

15. Leading through with a good climber A B C D E Having someone to share or even take the main responsibilities but technically trying to do your share of leading on the harder pitches is a good way of easing into the big routes.

CONCLUSION

Once you can lead safely on big cliff V. Diff's your progress depends much more on your fitness and enthusiasm than on any other factor. It is worth remembering that if you do not climb often, you will not each time be able to take up where you left off but will need to restart as a second or on easier climbs until you recover both the physical and the mental fitness needed to climb steep rocks.

Choice of climb is always the most important factor. It is easier to lead routes you have done before or those situated in areas you have walked in previously than to climb well in a strange area. Always treat guide book standards with respect, for different areas have different standards. Early leads are best made on low sunny crags which are popular. The presence of other climbers or nail scratches and litter (unfortunately) will indicate the route and many of a leader's problems will be solved. Do not be afraid to ask others for information or advice but do not always accept it blindly, especially if their climbing style, equipment and rope work is inferior to yours!

Leading gives the real thrill of rock climbing but also it is the least tolerant of errors. Whymper in the nineteenth century advised all climbers to 'look well to each step'. This advice is applicable especially to the steps involved in becoming a rock-climbing leader.

DOWN, UP AND ACROSS WITH THE ROPE

So far the climbing rope has been considered only as a safety factor for leader and second but there are occasions, at all stages in your climbing career, when the rope can be used to help progress down, up or across blank areas of rock. These are specialised skills needing practice and they will fit into your overall development as a rock climber at different stages.

I. DOWN WITH THE ROPE

CLIMBING DOWN
In Chapter VI, the methods of climbing down rocks were described. If roped, the leader (the most experienced climber) would come last, being protected if necessary by runners placed by the climber immediately ahead of him. On hard moves he could leave a short sling runner over a spike above him and flick it off with the rope once he was down the section. If in real difficulty he could leave a thread runner or a chock and karabiner and untie from the rope once down and pull it through, sacrificing the equipment. The advice for all descents is that when in doubt, play safe and abandon your gear despite the cost. After all, your life is much more valuable.

ROPING DOWN
On harder faces, climbing down is too slow and difficult and *roping down* or *abseiling* is a much more enjoyable and quicker method. The fundamental system is for the rope to be doubled and looped over a firm spike of rock or through a belay sling or piton. The climbers slide down the double rope controlling

their speed with friction either around their bodies or through some mechanical device. Once down, one end of the rope is pulled and the other end allowed to go free until all the rope is recovered.

ABSEIL POINTS

The first stage is the selection of the abseil point. The ideal abseil anchor should be absolutely solid with no possibility of the rope or sling rolling off it. It should be high above the starting ledge and it must be possible to retrieve the rope by pulling it once you are down.

Although the load on an abseil point should not be as great as the possible load on a main belay, the climber cannot avoid putting some load on it. All the tests needed to select a belay anchor should be used and if you are in any doubt, you must use extra anchor points until you are absolutely certain. Abseiling accidents are invariably serious. They often involve both climbers, and almost without exception have been caused by failure at the anchor point.

When using a sling through multiple belay points, make sure each one is tied off individually so that if one fails, the abseil rope is allowed neither to go free nor to move down thus shock-loading the remaining points. The sling should be in good condition.

Many dodges are possible to protect the sling from damage or to facilitate the recovery of the rope. Sharp edges should be padded or rounded off, and sharp bends in the rope avoided by using long slings on the abseil point. The rope should be threaded through so that the inside half is the one to pull, thus minimising friction due to pinching (58).

One final danger arises from the use of old slings found in regular abseils. These are often weak or rotten and usually it will pay to replace them. Never blindly trust other people's knots or abseil anchors.

THROWING DOWN THE ROPE

Having selected the anchor it is necessary to get the rope down in the right direction without a tangle or a knot in it. If you are both on a small ledge, attach yourselves to a separate belay anchor using slings clipped directly into your belts before you unrope and prepare the abseil.

58. Abseil sling used on angular spikes to ensure rope recovery. The lower inside rope would be the one to pull. Note middle mark.

59. Abseil ropes joined using figure of eight knots and a screwgate karabiner.

With just one rope it is possible to find the middle, if you have not marked it, as you thread it through. A long double rope has each half a different colour and presents no problem, but two separate ropes need joining. Either tie a figure-of-eight knot in each end and clip them together with a strong screwgate karabiner (59) – this is quick and presents less problems with knots jamming than you would expect – or join the ropes with a double fisherman's knot (Chapter v) with the ends protected by full hitches. Throw each half of the abseil rope separately but in the same direction. It often pays to feed down a loop from the abseil point as far as possible and then to throw the remainder in small coils out from the crag, for any attempt to throw all the rope in coils will result in a tangle. Alternatively, if the position is not suitable for this technique, build up a pile of rope from the abseil point on the ledge at your feet and then throw just a few small coils, letting these small coils drag the rest of the rope off the ledge from the top of the pile. In some situations it is worth putting knots in the ends of the two lengths to stop a careless abseiler from going off the end, but if this is done it can cause the rope to tangle or jam and also it makes separating the ropes more difficult.

ABSEILING METHODS
There are three standard methods of abseiling. One uses just the rope, one uses the rope with a sling and karabiner and the most comfortable uses rope, sling, karabiner and a device known as a descendeur.

a. Classic abseil (60)
For this method, the climber stands astride the doubled rope facing the abseil point. He lifts it up from behind with the right hand, passes it across his chest, over his head and onto

60. Classic abseil.

61. Standard abseil. Method of clipping in the rope gives slightly increased friction.

his left shoulder. He retakes it with his right hand held near the back trouser pocket. The left hand holds the ropes between the climber and the abseil point at about face height. Now the climber walks backwards down the face trying to keep his feet flat on the rock. The right hand, by moving forward, increases the friction whilst the left hand is used only to keep the climber in balance. One major mistake is to hold too tightly with the upper (left) hand. This is wrong whichever method you use. It is also important to keep the rope well under the right thigh, up to the buttock if possible and to keep the right leg lower than the left. If the right leg is allowed to go too high, then the rope can slip down to behind the knee with disastrous results. However well you use this method, it can be painful and it is not recommended for long abseils or beginners.

b. Standard abseil (61, 63)

For this method you need a one-and-a-half-inch wide tape sling about ten feet in length (depending upon your hip size) and a screwgate karabiner. Put the sling on rather like a nappy. Hold the sling behind your back with both hands,

62. Tape sling with screwgate clipped in.

then, holding the sling, slide both hands round to the front. Now hold the two loops thus formed with one hand, with one strand tight behind the back (this is the place for any knots) and one loop hanging down. With the other hand collect this loop from between the legs and clip all three loops together in front of you (62). This method is better than using a shorter sling twisted into a figure-of-eight with one leg being put through each loop, because it gives back support as well.

63. Controlling friction in standard abseil: stopping.

Again, stand astride the two abseil ropes. Clip them into the karabiner, which then is screwed up and the screw turned away from the rope. Place the ropes over one shoulder, diagonally across your back and hold them at trouser pocket height with the opposite hand, so with the rope over your left shoulder, your right hand controls the friction and your left hand just helps you to keep your balance. Now walk backwards down the rock, heels against the face, legs straight and slightly apart, body fairly upright. Try to keep clothing and long hair away from the karabiner, in fact, before starting tuck away anything that may catch. It is a good idea to wear gloves for abseiling and to pad the shoulder to guard against rope burns, particularly on long, free (overhanging) abseils on 9mm rope.

c. Descendeur abseil

Many devices are available to create friction and thus spare the climber's shoulders and clothing, but they often kink the rope, get hot and melt the rope if the abseil is fast (as can the karabiner in b). It is possible to make an abseil device out of two crossed karabiners (a karabiner brake), but one of the best and simplest descendeurs is made in the shape of a figure-of-eight. The large, thick figure-of-eight descendeur of alloy (not the thinner, lighter one) gives adequate friction and is large enough to conduct heat away. The device is placed on the ropes by holding it like a frying pan, passing a loop down through the large hole and then looping it over the handle part so that the ropes follow a U shape (64). Clip the smaller hole into your seat karabiner and abseil as usual (65). This can be locked by lifting the free rope over the top of the descendeur and letting it jam between the tight rope and the device (66), leaving the climber with both hands free.

SAFETY PRECAUTIONS

Various precautions can make abseils less dangerous. In order to load the abseil point as little as possible, try not to start by leaning out straight from it but sneak over the edge of the ledge on your knees or even by sitting and sliding off slowly (67). The biggest load on the abseil anchor comes in the first few feet, so try to keep the load at this time to a minimum. When abseiling it is a big temptation to go down in great

64. Descendeur clipped into rope.

65. Descendeur in action.

66. Descendeur locked with right hand.

67. Sneaking over the edge with poor low belay.

leaps and bounds. Each time you stop the anchor gets a shock load so it is much safer to aim for a smooth, controlled descent.

One other safety precaution is worth considering for every abseil. This is a top rope (or *safety rope* (68)). Always use a safety rope with beginners and whenever you doubt the anchor or the abseiler's equipment or technique. When giving a safety rope it is vital to use an independent belay. Often it is possible to fix another belay that, whilst not ideal as an abseil point, is perfect for a normal anchor. The safety rope should be attached to the abseiler's belt on one hip, well away from the abseil ropes. If two of you are faced with an abseil and are not completely sure of the abseil anchor, use a good separate belay anchor and a top rope. Let the heavier of you abseil first, bouncing and really loading the abseil point while he is protected. Then the lighter climber can abseil very gently. However, if you have any doubts, sacrifice more equipment, tie all the belays together and then both abseil gently. Two ways of safeguarding the last abseiler are possible. The safety rope can be clipped by the previous person into stopper runners placed down the line of the abseil, whilst an unprotected abseil can be made a little safer by tying a prusik knot (70), directly onto the abseil ropes and attaching this to your belt (69), You can slide this knot down with the upper hand but you must unhand it in emergencies. Sometimes climbers do not use a safety rope because of rope shortage. In this case it is possible to abseil on a single rope tied temporarily to the abseil anchor and to use the other half as a safety rope paid out by a companion belayed using slings.

RECOVERING THE ROPE

Many enjoyable abseils are spoilt by the rope jamming during recovery. Much of the success of this stage depends on the initial selection of the abseil point and the adjustment of the slings etc on it. Once one person is down the abseil, it is worth separating the two ropes, untwisting them if necessary and having a trial pull from below to see if the rope can be recovered. When this has been done, the climber below should keep the two rope ends apart. When everyone is down, separate the rope ends by about twenty feet and then by

68. Abseiler protected by safety rope attached to belt.

69. Prusik sling used to stop abseiler.

flicking and shaking ensure that no twists exist out of view. Finally, slacken off the free end and pull smoothly on the other. 'Snakes' sent up the freed rope can help movement to start, for often it is just the weight of this rope resting on the rock and the sling that causes friction. Always persevere with the flicking and gentle treatment before everyone starts heaving on the rope. As the end approaches the sling, do not snatch or increase the speed but let the weight of the pulled rope ease the end through and drag it down to you. Any excessive jerking in this final stage could cause the trailing end to wrap round the pulled rope or to lash out of the sling and flick behind a flake or round a spike. So be gentle. Finally, as the rope comes down, duck under cover to avoid any stones swept off the abseil ledge. Of course you could have anticipated this danger and moved any loose stones to a safer place before you started your abseil.

DANGERS
Many famous climbers have died abseiling, for the dangers are numerous and sometimes difficult to avoid. They can be divided into those caused by the rock and your equipment and those due to your technique. Those in the former category need thought and sometimes expense to be sure, whilst abseiling practice in a safe place, protected by a top rope, is a vital stage in the building up of good technique.

LOWERING-OFF
In certain situations, you may have perfect anchors but be very unsure of your companion's ability to abseil. In this case it is better to lower him. Put him into a seat as for the standard abseil (b) and clip the seat into the normal figure-of-eight knot on his climbing rope, which is attached also to his climbing belt. Place the rope from him through a descendeur attached directly to the abseil point and (using a separate belay anchor), lower him down the crag. He should walk backwards as though abseiling and can hold the rope above him with both hands for security and confidence. You should pay out the rope smoothly using a waist belay. If you are dubious about the abseil anchor, stand belayed above the descendeur so that you take as much weight as possible on your back and legs and

only use the device to absorb a little of his weight. This technique is useful also in a rescue situation with slightly injured companions, and may be of value when faced with an abseil in cloud or in wind too strong to throw the ropes.

2. UP WITH THE ROPE

Sometimes climbers need to climb up the rope. Occasions vary considerably but the original method was evolved in the Alps so that a climber who fell into a crevasse on a glacier could use the rope, belayed by a companion, to get out again. Today these techniques are used on rock climbs. When a climber falls on overhanging rock, he hangs free and must get back on to the rock. When abseil ropes jam, one end must be secured and the other half climbed. Climbers who descend from half completed artificial climbs (Chapter IX) usually find that it is easier to leave the rope and return up it to continue the route. On really big artificial climbs, the second may follow by climbing up the rope depegging the pitch as he does so.

Two methods are worth learning. One involves only normal climbing gear and the second uses a mechanical device.

PRUSIK-KNOT TECHNIQUE

The prusik knot (70) is a hitch made with a loop attached to the main climbing rope. When the knot is loose it can be slid up or down by hand, but as soon as pressure is applied it tightens round the climbing rope and jams firmly. It must be made with slings of a smaller diameter than the rope, although tape loops also can be used. If it slips, pass an extra turn through to increase the friction. In any situation where a

70. A prusik knot.

71. Ascending with jumars.

climber may find himself hanging free, he needs to be wearing a seat rather than the normal waist belt. Three prusik slings are needed. Two long ones are tied to the rope at face height and then are taken round each leg and on to each foot. Now, in theory, the climber can stand in one loop and whilst hanging from one hand holding the rope, he can slide the other loop up the rope, then he steps up into this loop and slides the lower knot up too. The strain on the arms is high, the body tends to spin, and the legs stick out in front. A third, shorter sling under the arms and round the back helps. It is attached to the rope by a separate prusik knot. Practice and experimentation with this method are necessary to get loops of the correct length and to develop a rhythmic technique (but the next method is far better).

JUMAR TECHNIQUE (71)
Various devices are manufactured to do the job of prusik knots. Some have built-in dangers, most have snags either of size and cost or design. Jumars are the biggest – two handles

which slide in one direction only, unless the ratchet-catch is opened. The basic prusik knot technique can also be modified. Two Jumars are clipped to the rope. The top one is attached direct to your seat sling or a harness by a screwgate karabiner and a short sling. With the correct length sling you should be able to dangle in your seat and still reach the Jumar handle comfortably. The lower Jumar carries a tape sling of such length that, when your foot is in it and your leg straight, the Jumar is below the waist. All the work is done by the legs so you could hang a second, equally long loop from the lower Jumar if you wished. Slide the lower Jumar up towards the upper one, bending the leg. Then straighten the leg and slide the upper Jumar at the same time – but not too far. If the end of the rope is not weighted (rucksack) you may need to hold the rope below the lower Jumar whilst you slide it up. Try to use the legs as much as possible and save arm strength. Once a rhythm is found, this method is quite fast and fairly easy. Many variations on these basic methods are possible and all are worth practising. Always practise with a top rope until you are sure of your method.

3. ACROSS WITH THE ROPE

In Chapter IX ('Artificial climbing') the technique of using diagonal abseils to cross blank rock is described. However, on some rock climbs it is necessary to traverse holdless sections horizontally or diagonally upwards. In this case a 'cowboy' technique can be used, lassoing a spike of rock using a sling or the rope, and then swinging across or climbing up. For lassoing with a sling, a long soft light loop is needed. Remove the karabiner to save your strength and then throw the sling upward to hit the rock above the intended spike. Your aim will be for it to tumble down on to the spike, and then you can adjust it by hand – you will be holding the sling with the knot in your palm. Flicking and lashing with a lasso works only on large spikes. When lassoing with a rope, the same technique can be used. Take more rope into your hand than you need and throw this bundle of coils to hit the rock just above the intended spike. It should drop down and at least one strand hook on the spike.

In the Alps, the most unclimbable pinnacles have been ascended using a lassoing method called a *Tyrolean*. Here the climbers ascend an adjacent face or tower, then lasso their summit and having secured the ropes, slide across – spectacular and exciting climbing. In British mountains this problem does not arise but the technique is used on sea cliff traverses. Crossing a zawn or cave in sea cliffs can involve either long, desperate traverses into the depths and out again or a short swim. If a rope can be fixed directly across, then the party can follow quickly and in the dry. It may be possible to lasso a large flake as described above, otherwise just one person can swim over. Another exciting method of getting a rope across is by loading one end with pitons, a hammer and chocks and swinging this bundle across into a crack or chimney or even a pile of boulders. Gentle pulling may cause it to jam.

Once the rope is across secure your end as high as possible and tension it only sufficiently for you to stay dry, remembering it will sag quite a lot with your weight. Sit in a seat and with the seat clipped to the rope, and wearing a back rope, lower yourself across. At the far end you will need to climb up the rope and a Jumar as a handhold may be useful. Once one person is across, the ropes can be properly secured with provision for pulling the end across once everyone is over.

SUMMARY
In these rope manoeuvres, as in artificial climbing, the climber must place all his trust and all his weight on items of equipment whereas in normal free climbing, equipment is tested only if the climber makes an error and falls. It is this fundamental difference which increases the risk. Whenever possible minimise this extra risk by using a safety rope. Thus protected, you can enjoy this valuable experience with ropes and gadgets. Many of these techniques need practice and often it is possible to get this, provided the belays are good, in gymnasia, on climbing walls and even on trees and buildings.

ARTIFICIAL CLIMBING

In normal climbing, the climber needs hand and foot holds to progress. On a big crag there may be a perfect line of cracks and slabs making an obvious route with one short unclimbable section. These short stretches can be climbed by the placing of *pitons* (*pegs*). These metal spikes are hammered into any cracks or holes that exist and the climber uses them as artificial holds, in some way, to make progress. Historically this is the basic form of artificial climbing on the mountain crags of Britain. On some climbs it is only necessary to have one or two pitons to climb across a blank section and then they can be used as hand or foot holds as in free climbing.

If the climbing is very steep or holdless it is usual to clip a sling into the piton and to stand in this for an extra foot hold. This is called an *aid move*.

The logical development of this occasional use of aid was for bigger cracks and walls to be climbed. These routes were considered quite impossible by ordinary means and so completely artificial pitches or even climbs have developed. Certain areas in Britain have been treated as purely artificial climbing grounds, notably big overhanging limestone walls and certain gritstone quarries. The tendency is to reduce the number of pitons and to try to climb these faces free. This development is due to the higher climbing standards of each new generation of leaders.

THE BASIC SYSTEM

The climbing of an artificial pitch involves three distinct phases. First the leader must know how to place pitons. Then he must use the rope and slings or ladders in order to move up as high as possible on each piton. Finally the second climber must follow, removing the pitons.

PLACING PITONS

When you drive in a piton, you must be aware of the type of loads you might place on it. For example, if you use a piton as your main belay then it will have to be the anchor which can withstand a full leader fall, taking the leader's dynamic load and the second's weight. Therefore it should be of similar strength to the rest of the belay chain, say 4,000lb. Similarly, if a piton is used as a stopper running belay, the loads could be equally as high. An aid-piton, however, may be needed to give only slight help and so has to support just your own weight or even part of your weight.

To summarise, pitons used for main anchors, protection and also for fast abseils need to withstand dynamic loads many times a man's weight. Those used for aid or gentle abseils are only statically loaded up to a maximum of twice the leader's weight.

It used to be believed that every piton, whatever its use, should be driven in to give maximum security. Often, on artificial climbs, this meant that pegs were overdriven. This deformed the peg, damaged the rock and made the piton irretrievable. This practice is very time-consuming and so skilled artificial climbers tend to place pitons with the minimum of time and effort, the intended loading being very clearly in mind. Obviously, a stopper piton or runner is needed every twenty feet as in free climbing, but the other pegs do not need to take very heavy loads.

The holding power of a piton depends on three factors – the quality of the rock, the material and design of the piton, and (most important of all) the skill of the person placing it.

Tests have indicated conclusively that pitons hold greater loads in hard rock than in soft rock. Also it has been confirmed that, ideally, the crack in which the piton is placed, should run at right angles to the predicted direction of strain. This means that a piton will hold much better in a horizontal crack than in a vertical one (72). Friable rock, cracks behind detachable blocks and expanding flakes considerably reduce the holding power of a piton.

A very wide range of pitons is available and nearly all are constructed of one of three materials – soft steel, alloy steel or wood. A well designed piton has several characteristics. It has a small eye close to the shoulder so that the distance between the karabiner and the edge of the crack is as short as possible (elliptical eyes greatly reduce holding power). It has a square shoulder so that it comes into contact with the rock allowing the minimum amount of bending. It also has a strong head that will not deform under loads or hammering and a blade of maximum rigidity in relation to cross-section and weight.

The condition of a piton is also very important. Soft steel pitons deform and rust and those found in place on climbs should be checked before being used. Hard steel pegs develop fatigue cracks with repeated use and must then be discarded.

Soft steel pitons rarely withstand large dynamic loads, because although they deform on insertion to follow the shape of a crack, they may pull out and deform with loads under 1,000lb. Hard steel pitons do not deform on insertion but damage the rock instead. These pitons will withstand quite large dynamic loads, particularly if placed in horizontal cracks. In vertical cracks, only the Z form hard steel pitons will sustain large loads. Pitons should be carried 'racked' like

72. Offset hard steel piton well placed on a horizontal crack.

chocks. It is better to use a bandolier sling although some climbers do carry them on their waist.

You can buy and carry the best pitons available but unless you place them correctly you may as well use old lumps of iron. Many of the skills of piton placing can be gained only by practice, and once again an occasional hour spent experimenting with pegs on a boulder can give valuable knowledge. Soft steel pegs can be hammered into the most unlikely crevices and holes, but hard steel pegs nearly always need a crack. With either type they should be selected so that they can be hammered in up to the head. In cracks, the piton should be placed in widenings so that rotation and leverage in the line of the crack is impossible. The more of the crack that grips the peg the better. Poor placing in which the peg is held at one point (a pivot) is very bad. If the correct piton has been selected, then it should be possible to insert about two-thirds of its length into the crack by hand (73). Z form pegs should be placed so that any load will rotate the peg with the two edges cutting into the rock (74).

73. Horizontal hard steel piton (Kingpin or Lost Arrow) inserted two-thirds by hand.

74. Z form peg (Leeper) loaded correctly.

Ideally a hard steel peg should be placed by hand and, after a few blows with the hammer, take a load of over a ton. Test it with a few light, sideways blows. If it does not move and the head is close to the rock, resist the temptation to hit it again. However, if it does move, drive it in a little more and test it again. In the interests of speed, preservation of the rock, preservation of your pitons and even holding power, one should not over drive a piton except in poor rock or with poor placements.

At this stage it is worth mentioning the hammer. For placing an occasional piton a light hammer is sufficient but for prolonged artificial climbing a heavier head is better. A hammer which also has a spike is very useful, especially for the second. The hammer should be attached to the climber's belt by a cord about three feet long and carried in a holster.

Sometimes a piton cannot be driven home its full length. In this case, to clip a karabiner into the eye would cause great leverage and so it is much better to 'tie off' the peg using a

77. Tying off iii: Threaded bong-bong.

76. Tying off ii: Larkshead.

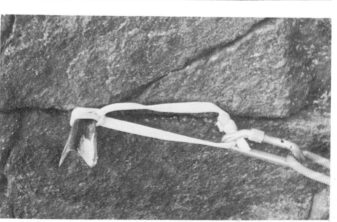

75. Tying off i: clove hitch – finally wrap sling once over peg.

short tape loop (*hero loop*). A *clove hitch* (75) or a *larkshead* (76) can be used for this. With big pitons (*bongs*) and wood wedges it is possible to treat the peg as a chock and thread round or through it (77). Sometimes you will not have a piton wide enough for the crack. In this case it may be possible to place two or more pitons side by side (*stacking*) to give some security. At other places, two or three poor pitons can be placed and tied together. Try to connect them so that they are all equally loaded and make sure that if one comes out, the sling and karabiner is still clipped into the others.

CLIMBING ON PITONS

Having either placed or reached a piton, the next problem is how to use it to the best advantage. The more continual the artificial climbing, the more sophisticated the system becomes. The range is from the single aid move on free climbs to the 300-foot walls of Yorkshire limestone. At the ultimate we have the American Yosemite big-wall climbs which need perhaps six days of climbing, involving the placement and removal of hundreds of pitons.

For the isolated aid-move it is simply a matter of placing two karabiners in the piton. Once you are sure the piton is good, clip the rope into the lower karabiner and pull up on the higher one. If the peg is dubious then it is better to clip in after you have pulled up. Some climbers like to get help from a piton by traction, that is by the second pulling them up to the peg using the karabiner as a pulley. This increases the load on the piton quite considerably and it is better, if traction is needed, to provide it yourself.

On steep climbs where many pitons are needed, the disadvantages of the standard waist tie (belt) become painfully obvious. A climber hanging free from his waist could be in trouble in a very short time so it is better to use a seat made from a tape sling as for abseiling or in the form of a commercially produced harness.

As in free climbing, it is possible to climb artificially using a single rope or a double rope. On straight cracks with pitons tied off to cut down rope drag, a single rope runs fairly well but otherwise it is better to use two ropes. Kernmantel ropes run more easily and kink less than laid ropes, so these are to be preferred. The leader on a single rope needs 150 feet of 11mm. When using double rope he can use either 300 feet of 9mm doubled or two separate 9mm ropes of 150 feet. For easier handling again, more strength (but also more weight), one 9mm rope of 150 feet and one 11mm rope of 150 feet can be used. Each system has its supporters but all agree that the two ropes should be of very different colours. Although it is possible to attach both ropes to the front of the harness it may be better to attach one to the harness and tie onto the second using the normal belt with its variety of positions.

In order to provide footholds you need to carry some form of ladder. Étriers are short ladders made of line with three or four metal rungs. They can be clipped into a piton direct using a karabiner or can be attached to griff-fifis instead. These are hooks with handles, and are attached to the climber by four feet lengths of cord and so it is possible to drag them up after you have left a piton. Nowadays, however, étriers are not as popular as tape ladders. These are lengths of inch-and-a-half tape tied into three or four loops. They are light and silent and the leader can carry half-a-dozen or more and leave them at strategic places up the pitch.

Finally, rather than clinging to each peg, as he reaches it, the leader needs some quick method of holding himself to it. The second can try to give this aid by hanging on the rope but this overloads the peg and exhausts the second. Rope stretch lets the leader sag anyway. It is better for the leader to clip himself to the peg either with a chain of karabiners or better, with a hook (fifi) on a short sling attached to the seat harness.

On a straightforward single crack artificial climb, the procedure is as follows. Place the first peg as high as possible. Clip a karabiner into it and into the karabiner (or the peg if possible) clip a pair of tape ladders on one karabiner. Place one foot in the bottom rung of one of the ladders and using both arms, pull upward to stand in the tapes, one foot in each tape. As quickly as possible, put your fifi hook into the ladder karabiner and sit back. Now clip the climbing rope through the other karabiner making sure it will run smoothly when you continue. Already things are complicated and it is possible to get ropes and tapes tangled. Many variations are possible on this first simple (?) step. Some climbers prefer to clip the rope into the piton before placing the ladders or moving up. This involves pulling up about six feet of rope and then asking the second to take in three feet as you move, but it also means that if the piton comes out then you have an extra six feet to fall before the load comes onto the lower piton. However, as some karabiners will not open once your weight is on them, this may be the only way to get the rope clipped in. The help of this temporary top rope can take some load off tired arms.

It is usual to clip in alternate ropes when using a double rope on straight cracks, hence the need for two colours. Bold climbers will reduce friction by clipping into stopper pegs or chocks only and by using the others merely for aids. A good system can be adopted by practice. Certainly no two climbers follow identical procedures, even up the same pitch. However, basic rules are worth keeping in mind and some tricks are possible. When looking at an artificial pitch, it is vital to imagine how the ropes, pitons and tie offs should look when you have finished the pitch. With a single rope it will be fairly obvious but with two ropes it is worth deciding on which side of you each rope should be, and then placing them accordingly. By looking up a crack you can estimate the size of piton needed and decide with which hand you will use the hammer, and so be able to have the pegs ready in the most accessible position. Similarly, you can have the appropriate *hero loops* ready. Tapes should be untangled and also hung in an accessible place. Often it is best to carry karabiners on a bandolier. Clip some singly, some in pairs, some with hero loops and some with pitons attached.

Strength can be conserved in a variety of ways. The weight should be kept off the arms as much as possible. As soon as the hook is in the peg, the climber must make a positive mental decision not to hang on with the hands but to let go and rest the arms. The only danger is that the peg could come out – and holding on to it will not prevent this from happening. Obviously the legs take some of the weight and rather than just standing in the ladders, you can adjust your position to provide better balance with less strain. On vertical walls it is often possible to stand in balance simply by putting the heels together and standing to attention. On overhangs, curl one leg up under you and sit on the heel to get a stable position. This is a manoeuvre for which tapes are far superior to étriers.

STANCES AND BELAYS

On normal, short artificial climbs ropework and belaying is the same as for free climbing but on big walls it may not be possible to find stances and so the leader must stop and take a hanging stance (a stance in slings). On pegged routes, stances normally have extra pegs and perhaps a foothold. If these are absent, the leader must decide when to stop. Rope drag or shortage of equipment may indicate the time to stop but ideally the leader should stance at a point where belay pegs can be placed in a good horizontal crack. It is worth putting a couple of pegs in the start of the next pitch so that both climbers don't have to hang from one peg. Alternatively, the second may step a few pegs below the leader and belay so that the leader can use his own belay pegs as his first stopper.

Both climbers can stance by just tying themselves to a peg and sitting in their harnesses but often it is better either to sit in tape ladders or to carry a canvas seat to clip into a couple of pegs.

As the climbers face into the rock, a normal waist belay is not possible and so it is usual for the leader to bring up the second by taking in the rope through a high peg and then using a waist belay or to take in directly round a figure-of-eight descendeur. When paying out to the leader, the second must pay out through a stopper peg and using either a descendeur or a waist belay across his body (78).

SECONDING ARTIFICIAL CLIMBS

The job of the second is often more tiring than that of the leader. On overhanging rock, the rope helps to hold the leader in but it tends to pull the second out. As soon as the second can reach the next piton he should unclip the rope from it, then clip in tapes and move up into them. Now he can sit down in the tapes with the loops pulled up to his thighs and maybe put his hook into a higher loop of the tapes. With his feet braced against the rock he is free to hammer out the

78. Leader and second on A1 climb. Note second's belays and leader's foot curl to rest.

previous peg. The correct way to remove pitons, particularly hard steel ones, is to hammer them as near the shoulder as possible. Hit them as far as possible in one direction and then a few blows more. Repeat in the opposite direction. Always stop before the peg starts to lose shape. If it does not come out, retap to the central position and it should be easy to remove. In some climbs in Yosemite, four hundred pitons have been placed and only two or three not removed. Pitons refuse to come out only if they are overdriven, or poorly placed, or if the remover lacks skill.

It is no use knocking out every peg on a route if you drop half of them, so sometimes it pays to have a short sling and old karabiner to clip into pegs before giving them their final taps. The second must rack the pegs in a similar fashion to the leader so that a rapid changeover can be accomplished.

GRADING

Artificial climbs are given grades according to difficulty but these seem to be even more variable than the grades given to free climbs. The grades are based on the following ideas.

'A1' pitches are rarely more than vertical with good rock and a choice of obvious peg placements. With pegs in place, these pitches may be possible without étriers or tapes.

'A2' pitches usually overhang. The line is not obvious and pegs often will be quite small and widely spaced, in pockets or poor cracks.

'A3' pitches involve poor rock, bad peg placements and continuous overhangs. The grade 'A4' is used sometimes to indicate the most overhanging and precarious type of artificial climbing with micro pegs etc. The addition of 'e' to the grade, ie 'A3e' shows that expansion bolts have been used.

Good descriptions give an indication of the number of pitons used on a pitch. *Topos*, an American idea, even give in diagrammatic form the type of peg needed as well. Always, the problem on British artificial climbs revolves around the question, 'What's left in?' On straightforward gritstone cracks you will be lucky to find more than an old battered peg or rotten wood wedge, but on some of the bigger limestone walls, lines of expansion bolts can be found, usually fairly rusted after a few winters. Local gossip or good binoculars are the only ways of getting answers. A pegged up route can be climbed quite quickly but a pegging ascent could take a full weekend.

OTHER AIDS
So far, various pitons have been mentioned, but other types of aid are also used. Some are ethically superior to pegs but one class, *expansion bolts*, are often the subject of controversy. These bolts are placed by drilling small, one inch deep holes in the rock and then fixing an engineer's bolt in place. Whilst giving a certain form of satisfaction to the leader on the first ascent, they give little pleasure to later parties other than as ladder ways.

Two other varieties of aid also exist. *Bashies* or *copper heads* which are lumps of soft metal on wires which can be hammered into hollows and pockets on the rock. In theory they deform rather than damage the rock. Bashies give very dubious security as do *sky hooks*, the final form of aid. These are rather like strong picture-rail hooks. They can be placed on small incut or flat holds and the climber can stand in a tape hanging from them. His weight keeps them on but as he moves, the hook usually falls off. The modern trend is to reject bolts and even to move away from pegs towards less permanent and damaging aids. Hence the use of artificial chocks instead of pegs is to be encouraged. The continual efforts to free climb previously artificial routes is a welcome trend.

TRAVERSES
A traverse on pitons along a horizontal crack is quite straight-forward, but the problem of getting from one vertical line of cracks to another without bolting is more interesting. On steep but not vertical rock, a tension traverse is possible with the second paying out the rope to your seat whilst you attempt a crab-like progress diagonally down towards the new crack. It may pay to descend vertically and then to pull across horizontally rather than to rely on smooth paying out by the second. On steeper rock, an abseil may be necessary from your top piton, again using a diagonal line on small side holds. The final resort is a great, galloping swinging pendulum running back and forth across the slab on an abseil until you

can grab the new crack. These abseils need to be done with some form of descendeur so that at least one and possibly both hands can be freed.

SUMMARY
Artificial climbing is very technical, and takes the climber into the most exciting situations on big walls and roofs. Often it is possible to reduce artificial climbs to your own standard. For the beginner, this is a useful factor, but your aim always should be to reduce the amount of aid you require and to try not to damage the rock face. The dangers of artificial climbing are often more apparent than real but falling from overhanging rock can create a major problem. The leader, and to a very great extent the second, may have real problems regaining contact with the rock and often it is not possible to lower the swinging climber to the ground. Jumars or prusiks and the skill to use them are essential in these cases.

The practice of artificial climbing will help your free climbing in two ways. You will learn to place pitons and to use the double rope more skilfully. Even if the thrill of the big walls and roofs is not attractive to you, some experience of this form of climbing is valuable and will enhance your overall skill as a rock climber. Artificial climbs will 'go' in any weather and give a concentrated type of pre-season physical training which can form a good base for the summer's free climbing.

HARDER CLIMBING

Many climbers are content to climb routes in the lower standards of difficulty, that is those routes graded up to Severe. There is no doubt that some of the most enjoyable routes in Britain are in this category and that there is little to equal the pleasure found in a full day of movement over a thousand feet of good steep rock. Before the war there were only a few Very Severe climbs in each area and only a handful of climbers who could lead these hard routes regularly. Now with modern footwear and equipment, Very Severe is commonplace and it is quite normal to see young leaders 'bombing' up routes of this standard and above. Although the techniques and methods so far discussed are basic to all climbing, at the highest standards various other considerations are involved.

ROPEWORK
Many of the hardest climbs ascend vertical or overhanging rock and the problem of a climber's *power to weight ratio* becomes critical. A climber with only normal arm and finger strength must be aware of the weight problem at all times and must be very selective with the equipment he carries. One major problem on hard routes is rope drag, for often running belays do not come in nice straight lines and so however carefully placed and tied off the runners are, the rope friction is still great. Therefore it is preferable to use double rope as for artificial climbing, preferably in two colours, and both of at least 9mm Kernmantle or No. 3 (1¼in) Hawser laid. Then a leader can plan how he will use each rope separately for running belays. Compare photograph 37 with photograph 35

79. Hard climbing. Tom Proctor on Green Death, unprotected climbing on **exceptionally** thin holds.

and 36. It is bad practice to clip both ropes through only one karabiner and this should be avoided. One other advantage of double ropes becomes obvious when one is cut through during a leader fall.

Skill with the rope is often vital if a leader on hard climbs is to get the rest of his party up the pitch after him. He can use one part of the double rope purely for his own protection and place runners on the other rope with the second's problems in mind, particularly on traverses. Generally it is not a very good practice to haul seconds bodily up routes. A ten pound pull on the rope at the crux is considered by most British professional guides to be the right amount of help to be given. If the second needs more than this, then the party should be on an easier route. On some occasions, however, the second may exhaust himself whilst trying to remove a well placed runner or piton and then may need a real pull. A deep knee bend by the leader accompanied by the taking in of a couple of feet of rope and followed by a smooth straightening up may help. Always warn the second so that he can help too. When you pull, discourage the second from holding the rope and persuade him to use rock holds or runners instead. If he insists on climbing the rope, secure one rope directly to the belay, using a prusik sling or tying it to an extra karabiner with a figure-of-eight knot, and let him climb this while you take in on the other rope.

On very steep climbs it is better to use a seat harness rather than just a belt. With double rope either attach both ropes to the seat or better, use a seat and a belt with one rope on each. It is important that at least one rope can be moved round the body to various positions both for belaying and protection.

CHEATING

One old climbing motto goes something like this. 'It is better to explain to your friends why you cheated than to explain to St. Peter why you didn't.'

There are many ways of climbing a given pitch and the exact mode of ascent is really only a matter between the climber and his conscience. Certainly the more pure the ascent, the more satisfying it can be. Some cheating does affect the climb for others and so the hammering in of pitons on free climbs, the hammering of artificial chocks so that they cannot be recovered and the chiselling of new holds should be avoided. Sometimes a sling, peg or chock needs to be left to facilitate retreat. This seems unavoidable and usually is treated with tolerance but the use of extra permanent aids to continue to climb a pitch is to be deplored.

These are fairly obvious ways of cheating but the less obvious methods are a more personal matter. They are tricks to have available in cases of real need but, one hopes, rarely to use. They fit into two categories, those which require the assistance of the second and those which are purely the work of the leader. In the first category lies the most common, the *leader's top rope*. On hard sections the leader continually places runners above his head and the second tensions him to them. Then the second can hold him in position while he rests both hands and places a higher runner. An extension of this is for one climber to climb so far up a pitch placing runners until he is exhausted, then he is lowered to the ground and his companion is hauled up to the top runner and continues fresh. This seems to be permissible on new routes (*varied leads*) but not on successive ascents. Even without the second's connivance, the leader can still lower considerably the standard of a given free climb by using his frequent *running belays for aid*. He can use them simply as handholds and pull on them or he can hang slings from them and stand in these. Finally, he can use *the third hand technique* and have a fifi hook or spare karabiner clipped into his belt to place in runners and so rest both his arms.

It would seem that each pitch has a certain 'par' score rather like a hole in golf. This 'par' would be the accepted way a pitch is climbed using sufficient runners to be reasonably safe but getting no aid from them unless the aid is permitted in the guide book or is local practice. A leader's aid should be equal to or lower than this par score whilst still keeping good style and staying safe. The use of extra aid should leave the climber with some feeling of disappointment and the intention to do a better ascent next time or to climb at a lower standard.

SOLO CLIMBING

A modern tendency is for the best climbers to climb solo as the purest form of climbing pleasure. In the days before running belays, leaders often used the thinnest hemp line as climbing ropes in order to save weight and so any fall by the leader was serious. The modern solo climber is in the same position. He can carry some protection if he wishes. He can wear his belt, place the odd chock or sling runner and clip himself to it using a long sling. In this way he can risk a short fall or can clip in and blow his whistle for help if he gets stuck. The purists do not do this, for all they carry is a couple of karabiners to clip into any aid pitons they may find. Solo climbing seems to be a direct reaction against the sophisticated safety equipment now available and the tedium this can create in a slow party. Climbing solo at high standards is for the few whilst soloing on lower standard routes still carries an element of risk due to objective dangers.

FITNESS

Climbing at the highest standards requires great physical fitness. In the past, climbers were proud to boast that for this sport they trained in the pub but the modern 'super tiger' needs superb physical strength as well as the mental confidence that many consider the main attribute. Careful dieting, moderation and plenty of sleep will improve the performance in this sport as in any other, whilst some form of fitness training is vital. The best training for climbing is climbing. Bouldering, rapid climbing on outcrops, following circuits, long hill days with plenty of walking and climbing are ideal. However, if you live in a city, then climbing walls, gymnasium work, weight training and some running or orienteering will all help. Mental rehearsal is also important. It is possible to study a hard climb in pictures, diagrams and in books until you really know it and then to think yourself up it so that you really believe you can climb it. Then if your research is accurate and you have built up sufficient confidence, the actual climbing of the route should not present too many problems.

ROCK CLIMBING EQUIPMENT AND ITS CARE

1. FOR THE FEET

a. Rock-climbing boots When buying boots look for: rigid vibram sole with fibreglass or metal stiffening plate, narrow welt, narrow toe for jamming, sewn in tongue, D rings and strong hooks, nylon laces. Uppers should have minimum stitching and the boots should be a close fit when wearing one thick and one thin pair of socks.

After use: wash or brush clean, remove all stones from cleats of sole and heel, polish with wetproof or silicone shoe polish. If wet, stuff with newspaper and dry slowly in a warm airy place. Do not dry with direct heat.

Before climbing: retighten laces and kick cleats clear of mud, etc.

b. Rubbers When buying look for: smooth sole, shallow toe, protective rubber rand, good laces going right to toe. Aim for a close fit with one pair of socks and try a variety of makes to discover the firm which makes them your shape.

After use: wash soles, check and change laces regularly, slowly dry out sweaty interiors.

To improve: strengthen sides with soft leather patches, dust soles with french chalk for hard pitches. (Usually rubbers are referred to by their trade names, PAs, Masters, RDs, Gollies, etc.)

c. Socks Use one pair of wool/nylon interlock stockings and an inner pair of thin nylon/wool. Experiment with socks in various combinations. Always remove all wrinkles from both pairs. Keep toe nails cut short to extend sock life, prevent bruising on descents in boots, and to make rubbers fit better.

d. Spare lace Use a spare lace as a draw cord in your rucksack.

e. Foot cloth Carry a small piece of old towelling to dry the soles of rubbers on hard pitches with wet patches or on muddy stances.

2. FOR THE HANDS
a. Fingerless mitts Use woollen mitts with strengthened palms for warmth and finger freedom. Fairly good for rope holding and adequate to climb in.
b. Leather gloves Use strong leather (industrial) gloves with long cuffs for rope handling and abseiling.

3. FOR THE HEAD
Crash Helmet A good helmet should be well secured to stay in place at all times, even during falls. It should protect the head from all possible blows, absorb impacts, allow full head movement and unhindered all round vision, be well ventilated and of reasonable weight. Helmets of BSI 4423 are the best but may be too heavy for some climbers. They give protection in falls whereas others are good only for deflecting falling stones and glancing blows. Helmet fitting should be adjustable so that it is possible to wear a thin balaclava under the crash hat in winter. Climbers' slang for crash helmet is 'bone dome' or 'hard hat'.

4. THE ROPE
a. For normal climbing 120ft–150ft (36m–45m) of No. 4 Hawser laid rope. 1¾in circumference (11mm diameter) made to BSI 3104 *or* 120ft–150ft (36m–45m) of 11mm diameter Kern-mantel rope made to UIAA specification.

Hawser-laid rope is made by British Ropes under the trade name Viking. Kernmantel rope is made by British Ropes and various continental firms sometimes incorporating the word Perlon.

b. For hard climbing and artificial routes Double rope should be of at least No. 3 Hawser-laid, circumference 1¼in; or 9mm Kern-mantel, to the usual standards.

Ropes should be stored in the dark without knots and tangles, middles should be marked with tape or a nylon dye and ends sealed with a flame or hot knife.

After use: ropes need gentle washing in cold water to

remove grit and careful checking for cuts and damage. Wet ropes should be dried uncoiled in a well aired place.

Discard any damaged rope and always after long leader falls.

5. THE BELT OR HARNESS
Wide variety available ranging from the simple belt by Troll through various chest and seat harnesses by Moac, Irvin, Edelrid, Karimore and Troll to the Whillans harness by Troll.

Always get correct size, look for guarantees of strength, study design and workmanship for weak points. Many belts give belay problems so consider this also. Normally good harnesses have instruction leaflets.

6. KARABINERS – KRABS OR SNAPLINKS
Main tie on and belay karabiners should be UIAA approved with screwgate. Look for strength at right angles to axis as well as along axis. Strength should be over 5,000lb (2300kg).

For stopper running belays use alloy 2500kg karabiners. For other running belays use alloy 1800kg or above.

After use check for loose or stiff gates. Oil the hinge, file off sharp edges, check alloy krabs for cracks and dents. Wash all karabiners in fresh water after use on sea cliffs. Discard any damaged karabiners.

7. SLINGS AND CHOCKS
Make up own sets by experiment and practice. Seal ends of slings and tapes with a hot knife. After use check tape knots, splices and other knots. Tie down ends with tape. Fix chocks to wires with Araldite or something similar. Check wires for frays. Discard frayed wires, snagged tapes and old slings.

8. PITONS
Buy hard steel pitons for belaying and stopper runners but use soft pitons as well for artificial climbs.

Alloy steel pegs rust at a much faster rate than those of mild steel. Hence they should be lightly rubbed with an oily rag and stored in a dry place. Check after use for fatigue cracks, usually found at the junction of eye and blade. Pitons used in sea cliffs corrode at a high rate. Pegs that have been hammered may develop sharp edges to the head which can snag and damage rope and tie offs. These should be filed off. When the point of a piton becomes ragged and sharp it should be filed or ground to a smooth radius. This is true especially of knife blades. Caution must be exercised when grinding so that the piton does not overheat.

9. HAMMER

Wide choice available. Select one with the head weight appropriate to its task, attach to your waist by a single length of line and carry in a holster. Check wooden shafts for damage and heads for looseness after continued use.

10. DESCENDEURS AND ASCENDERS

The best device for abseiling, friction and mountain rescue is a figure-of-eight descendeur. Minimum breaking strain can be as large as 15,000lb. Made by Clog and others.

For ascending ropes (prusiking) various devices are available. Jumars are the most expensive, safest and easiest in use but they are also the bulkiest for they have handles. Cloggers are smaller and cheaper but require the climber to unclip them from the slings etc for some manoeuvres. They have no handles. Salewa or Hiebeler prusikers are light and simple but liable to come off the rope unexpectedly.

11. OTHER ASSORTED EQUIPMENT

a. For general climbing
A whistle carried in an accessible place.
A small sharp penknife.
A threader made of coat hanger wire.

b. For hard routes
Some climbers add a small bag of french chalk which they can use to dust their palms and sweaty hand holds. Sky hooks. Straight or curved on short tape slings. Fifi hooks attached to the waist belt with a small krab or short sling used to hook into pegs etc! (The third hand.)

c. For holding leaders

Sticht plate. A device to be used, either direct onto a belay anchor or attached to a waist belt or harness, to replace the second's body as means of holding falls. However, Italian hitch on a karabiner is just as good.

12. BASIC HILL WALKING EQUIPMENT

Consider carrying in your rucksack some or all of the following.

Map (1in or 2½in)	Gaiters
Compass – Silva	Head torch
Altimeter	Poly Bivy Bag (one or two man)
Waterproofs	Water bottles, flask
Extra sweaters	Spare food, batteries etc
	First-aid kit

Appendix I

MOUNTAIN RESCUE

Despite every precaution, rock-climbing accidents do occur, and it is every climber's duty to know how to call for help.

Mountain rescue in Britain is a free and purely voluntary service. The Mountain Rescue Committee (now registered as a charity) was formed in 1933, and is responsible for establishing rescue posts at strategic points.

There are more than 70 mountain rescue posts in Britain, some unmanned and providing a simple kit box only, others with several stretchers and first-aid rucksacks and a rescue team on standby at weekends.

The police are the main co-ordinators of mountain rescue, and through them can be summoned extra help – search dogs and other rescue teams, including the RAF and helicopters.

The National Health Service pays for the basic first-aid kit (stretcher, sleeping bags and first-aid rucksacks), but many other items are required, particularly at the busier posts. Money to buy extra radios, ropes and other equipment comes as voluntary donations—from climbing clubs, individuals, sometimes from accident victims or their relatives.

Full details of rescue posts can be found in the Handbook of the Mountain Rescue Committee, obtainable from the Secretary, 9 Milldale Avenue, Temple Meads, Buxton, Derbyshire SK17 9BE. This handbook is essential for all rock climbers (see also Appendix ii).

In emergency act quickly. Go to a rescue post or phone 999 and ask for the police.

Appendix II

FURTHER READING

Mountaineering is rich in literature. New books appear every year, particularly autobiographies and expedition reports, and they are often available at climbing shops as well as bookshops. Many of the older publications are out of print, so look for bargains in the secondhand shops.

1. INSTRUCTIONAL BOOKS

Mountaineering, by A. Blackshaw. Penguin Books, n.e. 1973. This excellent work contains much information about the whole sport of mountaineering both in Britain and abroad. It has a detailed and valuable bibliography.

Safety in Mountains, Central Council for Physical Recreation. Essential information for all mountain users.

Climbing in Britain, by J. E. Q. Barford. Penguin Books, 1946. op. The predecessor to Blackshaw, but still of interest to rock climbers as an indication of changes in both technique and attitude.

2. MAGAZINES

Mountain, ed. K. Wilson. 30 Collingwood Avenue, London N10. A top British mountaineering magazine, containing information about climbing at home and abroad.

Mountain Life, ed. C. Brasher. The Navigator's House, River Lane, Petersham, Richmond, Surrey. A bi-monthly journal supported by the British Mountaineering Council, free to members, with a wide general appeal.

Rocksport, 161 High Road, Chilwell, Nottingham. Concerned principally with rockclimbing in Britain.

Climber and Rambler, 56–57 Fleet Street, London EC4. Of general interest to walkers and climbers.

3. MOUNTAIN RESCUE

Mountain Rescue Techniques, by W. Mariner. Osterreicherischer Alpenverein. This book deals with standard continental rescue techniques.

International Mountain Rescue Handbook, by H. MacInnes. Constable, 1972. Details of all advanced rescue systems.

Improvised Techniques for Mountain Rescue, by B. Marsh. Jacobean Press. Basic techniques for rescue without a stretcher.

Mountain Rescue, Training handbook for the RAF, issued by the Ministry of Defence, 3rd edition 1972. Good basic advice on stretcher lowering, etc, which all rock climbers should study.

INDEX